MW00943215

Life Came to a
STANDSTILL

True Accounts of Loss, Love, and Hope

"Stories can lighten the darkness by making rainbows.
Such is the power and relevance of the
stories in *Life Came to a Standstill*."
—Dr. Hoi F. Cheu, Laurentian University

GWENDOLYN BROADMORE

www.gwendolynbroadmore.com

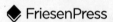

FriesenPress

Suite 300 - 990 Fort St
Victoria, BC, V8V 3K2
Canada

www.friesenpress.com

Copyright © 2017 by Gwendolyn Broadmore
First Edition — 2017

All rights reserved.

No part of this publication may be reproduced in any form, or by any means, electronic or mechanical, including photocopying, recording, or any information browsing, storage, or retrieval system, without permission in writing from FriesenPress.

There are multiple permissions, in place: regarding quotes, poems, and articles. Please refer to the "permissions page".

ISBN
978-1-5255-1282-7 (Hardcover)
978-1-5255-1283-4 (Paperback)
978-1-5255-1284-1 (eBook)

1. SELF-HELP, DEATH, GRIEF, BEREAVEMENT

Distributed to the trade by The Ingram Book Company

Dedication

To our loved ones, in gratitude for the gifts they have given us. We pay tribute to: Liam, Alan, Adrian, David, Russell, Sean, Brenda, and Robin. Each life is unique and irreplaceable—there is only one you.

Dedicated to every heart impacted by loss.

Permissions

Printed with permission from the contributing writers in *Life Came to a Standstill*, as follows: *Alan's Story*, Carol Reid-LeClair; *Adrian's Story*, Helen Jay; *David's Story*, Janet Rice; *Russell's Story*, Beverley Ogus; *Sean's Story*, Kathleen Stevens; *Brenda's Story*, Susan Massey; *Robin's Story*, Marjorie Suzanne (Suzy) Richardson.

Excerpts from "Some People," by Flavia Weedn: reprinted with permission from Richard Weedn, Archivea Inc., independent licensing agency for Archivea GmbH, copyright owner.

"Desiderata," by Max Ehrmann (1927): reprinted excerpts in *Liam's Story* and in its entirety in "A Poem Break."

"Window Washer Sings at the Terminal" and "The Ritual," from *The Red Element*, Insomniac Press, 2008: reprinted with permission from the poet, Catherine Graham.

"Six Healing Prayers" from self-published booklet "Art and Poetry by Kelly Foxton:" reprinted with permission from poet and artist Kelly Foxton, Nova Scotia.

"Good Night, I Love You, See You in the Morning": permission to reprint Robin's poem granted by her parents, Don Richardson and Marjorie Suzanne Richardson, who retain the rights to the poem.

Helping Yourself Heal When Someone Loved Dies, by Alan Wolfelt, Ph.D.: permission to reprint, Dr. Wolfelt (www.centerforloss.com) and through Bonnie Goss, Publications Editor, Companion Press.

The Myth of Closure: reprinted with permission from the author, Ashley Davis Bush, LICSW.
www.ashleydavisbush.com

We Choose to Read: Bibliotherapy and Memories of Loss and Grief: reprinted with permission from Hoi F. Cheu, PhD.

Table of Contents

Introduction

*"Give sorrow words; the grief that does not speak
whispers the o'er fraught heart and bids it break."*
—William Shakespeare, *Macbeth*

Please speak of your pain. A burden shared is a burden lightened. Welcome to our collection of eight true stories: real experiences written by the seven bereaved mothers and one bereaved sister who are living them. It is our belief that sharing will help you feel less alone.

If you have chosen to read *Life Came to a Standstill* following the death of your child, sibling, or another precious loved one, I am so sorry for your loss. If you have elected to learn more about grief in order to bolster a bereaved relative or a friend, thank you.

∞

A child's death is a displacement in the natural order of life. As the bereaved, we have unwillingly joined a terrifying club. It can feel as if the universe has betrayed us. Following my son Liam's traumatic death, it was alarming for me to see my image in a mirror. I could not meet the eyes of the hollow mask staring back at me.

The goal of *Life Came to a Standstill* is to provide you with support from those who are walking the path ahead of you. While marking the safe trails, we will point to a secure foothold here, a potential pitfall there. We strive to present coping tools from the hearts of many mentors, validation you can lean into.

There are no timelines for your journey. Give yourself permission to grieve and mourn in your own space and time. It may take years to find a true measure of who you are without your loved one's presence in your life. This is a part of your new normal. Please have faith that you will learn to live with your pain and value what remains.

You may feel achingly fatigued by raw emotions, making it difficult to visualize how to survive your sorrow. Trust that you can; believe that you will. Living one day at a time is a positive choice. It is calming to hold yourself firm to the present moment rather than letting your thoughts rebound unrestrained between memories of yesterday and imaginings of tomorrow.

Although your loss, indeed every loss, is unique, commonalities exist within grief. And the continuing effort you make to cope with and understand this bereavement journey is called grief work. It is the hardest work you likely will ever do, but it is crucial to attempt it otherwise you run the risk of staying frozen in pain and bitterness.

You may not recognize the expression "grief work" even if you have experienced grief. Many of us have suffered the sadness of loss. However, it is my feeling the death of an especially close loved one—one who resides within the intimate circle of your heart and your life—is the heaviest loss to face. It presents too challenging a road to walk alone. Please reach out for what you need.

It is natural to experience waves of confusion, and fear, when stomach-wrenching emotions control your world. These feelings are powerful. They may include: despair, fatigue, anger, sadness, yearning, anguish, disbelief, guilt, regret, shame, and blame. You are not going crazy, nor are you alone. Regrettably, during this nightmare, rollercoaster rides of misery are common. Furthermore, when someone within your innermost circle has died traumatically and without warning, shock and denial may last longer than you thought possible. In certain circumstances, you can suffer symptoms of post-traumatic stress disorder. Please speak to your health care professional about this.

What is grief work?

As I have experienced it, a vital component of grief work consists of granting oneself permission to grieve, with no apology for expressions of loss, including tears. Another important aspect is exploring any available road maps for this unfamiliar wasteland. With grief, maps have a variety of appearances and structures. Some guides are found in grief books and support groups. Other paths can be discovered through a knowledgeable grief therapist, a place of worship, a family doctor or other health care professional, and/or a special mentor.

Choices are diverse. They may include seminars on grief, attendance at trauma support centres, or participation in yoga classes to quiet the voices in your head. Journaling may draw fragments of your pain out of your mind onto a written page.

You choose.

You will sense which combination of resources nurtures you. The essential part is not to give up. Although it is tough work, each positive step will help buoy your strength and confidence. Be gentle with yourself and others. Remember that coping with the death of your loved one is a *process*, not a destination.

The support of family and friends remains invaluable. At first, their comforting familiarity may be all you can endure; even so, as soon as you are able, reach out further. Those who love us care deeply. Enduring personal grief, they try to grasp ours, yet in time our special people may attempt to recapture the person they once knew. If we are diverted enough, they imagine we will become okay, we will return.

Alas, this is magical thinking.

Distractions are valuable, soothing us with respites from grief. Nonetheless, the lifeblood for most of us is to have sanction to share our loved one's story again, and again. To be unable to can resemble a second death, the disremembering of one so near and dear to us.

Our family and friends may not get it. It is tough for them to comprehend that we are changed *forever*. It is not their fault. Recognizing the full scope of grief may not be possible without having walked the same path.

∞

Thank you for selecting *Life Came to a Standstill*. Although these stories each stand alone, they have been called chapters. The chapters were included in the order they were submitted; there is no additional meaning to their positioning in the book. I see them very clearly: chapter one, right through to chapter eight, as stepping-stones in a journey of grief, reconciliation, and hope.

The deaths of our loved ones were traumatic and unexpected: Liam and Brenda died by homicide, Adrian in a tragic car accident. Alan, David, and Russell died by completed suicide, Sean by what was thought to be an accidental drug overdose—but which turned out, possibly, to be suicide—Robin, suddenly and tragically, from a fatal blood clot. The time since these tragedies occurred ranges from two years to twenty-five years. Each loss is profound, and the grief paths are individual—as are the writing styles of the authors.

Introduction

I encourage you to read all eight narratives and continue to the insights waiting for you in the addendum. There may be some pages that speak more directly to your loss than others. Nonetheless, commonalities—in the experience of grieving—arise throughout the book, which may lend you a broader view of grief, life, and, in turn, of your own journey.

— Gwendolyn Broadmore

Chapter One

Liam's Story

Gwendolyn Broadmore

Liam Spencer Broadmore:
November 27, 1966–October 12, 2005

*You are a child of the universe
no less than the trees and the stars;
you have a right to be here.*
—Desiderata, Max Ehrmann

Liam's Story

The instant we returned to the empty cottage, our eyes latched onto the pulsing message light. We were out of sorts. From the beginning, this day had felt all wrong. We blamed our irritability on pre-winter clean-up, rarely an uplifting task, following Thanksgiving. We were keen to be home. It became an aggravation to backtrack with flooring samples—our fault, since we had succumbed to the lure of a fall clearance sale. Very soon, this everyday errand would recall a place of innocence, a place to which we would never return.

Phone messages at the cottage are rare at fall closing, but here was Liam's dad asking for *Erwin*, not me, to call him as soon as possible—alarm bells! Surely Liam must be home, in Stratford and at work by now. He left the cottage last night, following a late dinner, phoning on the way as promised.

Straight away, Erwin was on the phone.

I bolted to the back deck. Despite overhearing no words, my heart feared that our lives were shattered. I paced and paced, then cautiously peered through the window. My husband had the phone glued to his ear, his face the colour of chalk. As I burst into the cottage, his eyes found mine. He whispered, "I am so very sorry."

Dear Lord, what does he mean?

Clearly, Erwin would not look so desolate if a minor family mishap had occurred. Instantaneously, my heightened fears

9

ricocheted unrestrained—between questions unasked and answers not wanted.

Hanging up, gently enfolding me, he uttered four hideous words: "Liam has been murdered." Lurching in terror, my stomach plummeted to the floor; my mind staggered in total disbelief.

"No, no—how, in God's name, can this be true?"

Pinned in position, I was fixed to black out, but my traitorous body refused to fall down. Numbing—like Novocain—shock grabbed an immediate hold. Real life slumped to the side, vaguely out of focus, as if we gazed through bubbled glass, speechless spectators to another poor soul's anguish. Life as I knew it had come to a standstill.

For hours, Liam's dad had tried to reach us—frantic, yet unwilling to leave his home until we spoke. In a last-ditch effort, he had left a phone message at our cottage.

On Liam's final journey, he was heading to his home in Stratford, and his work, in technical support, for a local manufacturing company. Tragically, he stopped at the wrong place at the wrong time. In the early morning of October 12, 2005, two men of no fixed address, known to the police, and accompanied by two women, beat our son. He lost his life at a closed gas station in the heart of downtown Orillia—a town we pictured as a safe cottage community.

Liam was neither aggressive nor was he prone to anger. He was a sailor, a skier, a musician, a talented computer geek, and a generous friend—an ordinary guy. Strong and able, he landed on his feet consistently in life—but not this time. With his truck still running, our son died there.

Within hours, four suspects were picked up, in separate police cruisers, and taken to the local Ontario Provincial Police (OPP) station.

Traumatized and panicky, desperate to be home to an imagined safety, how were we to endure one hundred kilometers of driving? The road loomed interminably. With our minds and bodies reeling, a primitive survivor's instinct took over. Before another step was taken, we needed to reach out. Erwin phoned our brothers and grown children. And in those frenzied moments, I called our friend Leonore. After relaying the unspeakable, I asked her to please phone other friends—poor Leonore.

Even functioning minimally flattened us. We had to go. On auto-pilot, bathed in an ice-cold sweat, we drove to Coboconk to return, as promised, the flooring samples. If Liam is truly dead, what on earth are we doing?

It's impossible to know how Erwin navigated. Rigid with shock, clinging to denial, we were mute, barring fitful and sporadic bursts: "This cannot be true! Please, it has to be a mistake! Surely murder cannot happen to ordinary people?"

Though we gulped two liters of water, we were as parched as the desert floor. Our parrot, Blue—ever the gleeful traveller and raucous chatterbox—uttered not one small peep. Somehow we made it home, opening the door to a ringing phone. Within minutes, the doorbell chimed and the house began to fill: neighbours and friends dropping off food, my brothers straight from work. One of Erwin's brothers, Theo, burst in—he had arrived from hours away. Our sister-in-law, Ksenia, commandeered the kitchen.

Concurrently, I was numbed down yet speeded-up, driven to change bed linen and begin the endless loads of cottage laundry. With purpose and reason suspended, impelled to run faster and faster, I could not sit. I could not talk.

Liam's dad arrived. Everyone spoke at once. My brothers agreed to go to Orillia in the morning to claim Liam's Ford Explorer.

Also, they would stand in at the arraignment of those men who had been charged with the second-degree murder of our son.

How could we comprehend such language? We blinked and awoke in an alternate universe.

Through this madness, I could tell Erwin had meant to go. He was resolved to stare those killers down. I was grateful to my brothers for going instead. I could not bear to be home alone—not yet. Laden with disbelief and the powerlessness of a victim's anger, my brothers Jeff and Harold must have suffered unimaginable distress on their trips to and from Orillia. As of October 12, the life of our family slipped from normalcy—shifting to a bleak and menacing place.

∞

Thanksgiving weekend we had stayed longer at the cottage to be with Liam, who had booked an extra vacation day. In the early afternoon, he had tossed me his shorty wetsuit, entreating, "Hey Mom, come on out for a sail." The wind blew frigid that day, so I hesitated to relinquish my snuggly blanket and the safe distraction of my book. But Liam, an eager sailor, looked so hopeful. Out on the lake, I reflected, "What do you enjoy about sailing? Is it the peace and tranquility?"

He grinned. "That too, but mostly it's the power of harnessing the wind, mastering a momentary control of destiny." That was yesterday. Now everything is smashed to bits. We subsist in this netherworld, too far down to touch consolation.

∞

No one knew when the coroner would release Liam's body—first he required official identification. His dad insisted on going, which was very brave. I could not tolerate the thought. Rather, in an automated daze, I patrolled the house, asking the universe for miracles, beseeching God for mercy.

Parents, grandparents, other relations, and friends are buried in Pickering. Liam's father strongly resisted him joining them there. Pickering was distant for mourners to travel back and forth. With an alien rage lurking beneath our skins, we were fixed to fight, prepared for battle. Mercifully, cooler tempers prevailed. It made sense to choose a local funeral parlour.

Liam had believed a good wake was tantamount to displaying love and respect; we could not deny him. Plucked from the Yellow Pages, Dixon-Garland Funeral Home, in Markham Village, guided us through this nightmare with compassion and grace.

In deepest shock, we selected a coffin. "Which one do you want?"

"None, I want none."

We chose the grave and conferred with a minister. The funeral would be the following Tuesday, visitation on Monday. In those cruel hours, I ached. I pleaded desperately, "Can anyone answer me, why?"

Forgetfulness plagued us. Consumed with panic, we lost focus and memory. Erwin grabbed notebooks—one for incoming calls, one for outgoing—to record every detail. With the help of call display, when the media phoned we were silent. We could not bear to speak.

It became impossible to eat, frightening to sleep. In the silence of night, Liam's final cries erupted in my ears. Behind a curtain of closed eyelids, personal videos repeated and recapped. How could I know that these images would play in my mind for months and years to come?

Heavy despair moved in as I negotiated to rewrite our lives and change this barren ending. Will you tell me—with what can I bargain back my boy?

Friends and family took over: Donna found sleeping pills, Claire brought soup, Maureen scrubbed bathrooms, and Lynn pulled out photos and picture boards. Brothers and sisters-in-law listened to the beginnings of eulogies, and so on and so on. Monday would not be delayed or denied.

We reached the funeral parlour early, delivering eight picture boards, to visit Liam in solitude. His glasses had been shattered on that final night, and retained as evidence. I gave him a pair of mine. Adjusting the frames to my son's face, the ice-cold impact of his death crumpled me to the floor.

Family and friends, acquaintances, neighbours, and colleagues trickled in—they swelled to unexpected numbers. Stories of Liam surrounded us; timeless rituals sustained and cushioned us. Liam's friend Brent displayed his photo album of two buddies growing up, unwittingly bruising our hearts while we relived their cheeky teenage posturing.

A stranger respectfully approached us, confiding that he worked for IBM Support providing online help to a whole range of companies, including Liam's. Among his tech responsibilities, Liam attended to his company's mainframe—as a result, they spoke often. This compassionate young man felt it imperative to share how very highly he thought of our son, and that he was already missing him acutely. This exchange became an essential moment, reinforcing how powerful caring, heartfelt words could be.

Another pal eagerly disclosed that it was because of Liam that he had his job. Following a day's work, Liam had stayed late into the night coaching Brian. Afterward, when the first interview bombed, Liam cajoled another one—a second chance. It worked.

The next day, eight heartfelt eulogies were dedicated to Liam. The minister advised us, "When you sense you are breaking down, speak louder. You can do this!"

I began, "Do not think me brave; this is the last gift I can give my son …"

If a funeral can be beautiful, this one was. So many looked to keep a hold of his memory, to express how Liam had made positive differences in their lives. He was a private guy—most of the stories we had known nothing of, until then.

More than one hundred people returned home with us.

Doubtless it is difficult to grasp the manifestations of shock that cause many bereaved people to appear more composed than they are. Some well-meaning acquaintances, with a need to console, complimented us on our strength, assuring us that in time we would be fine. Instinctively, I nodded. Yet mutinous in my heart and soul, I questioned in silence, "Would *you* feel this way if Liam was *your* child?" Of course, they did not know this, but at such a time it is best to say "I am so sorry," or no words at all … simply hold my hand.

"What restraint or limit should there be to grief for one so dear?" —Horace

Splintered and broken, we had no protective casts to shield our hearts and minds. The funeral was over; now what can we do? The way Liam died impeded our ability to grieve. Mental images of his precious life, violently and sinfully snuffed out, infused us with rage and thoughts of revenge. We were reassured that neither were we crazy nor were we alone in our terror and wrath. Surely wanting to rip my face from my body cannot be normal? Just the same—in some cultures it is customary for the deeply bereaved to rend their clothing and tear their hair, wail and keen. This was me! I needed this to be me! Instead, I allowed decorum to clamp on restraints.

∞

When a loved one has died by homicide, it is usual for grief and mourning to be delayed until those responsible are brought to some kind of justice. We survived walking from moment to moment, breaking each day into miniscule pieces, with manic attention to lists. Demands persisted, despite our lack of confidence or strength for commitments of any kind.

Our circle of life cracked wide open while the world outside our doors barely hiccupped. We hid from whatever we could. But the OPP Homicide Unit had already delayed our statements until after Liam's funeral. No more hiding. For the sake of the criminal investigation, detectives came to our home, recording our testimonies with compassionate respect. Erwin asked questions and took notes.

Powerless to sit in one spot long enough to absorb any words, my despair was too raw for me to hear or bear. Upon leaving, the detectives assured us: "These accused men will not be granted bail." We experienced a fleeting rush of relief.

By postponing appointments with the Crown attorneys and their teams until the New Year, we prayed we would glean the strength to cope. We had absolutely no understanding of criminal law, but came to know that, in Canada, the Crown prosecutes on behalf of the government. What about us? Do we have rights, as surviving victims? How can we ensure justice for Liam? We needed to pinpoint this and more.

With our trust decimated, we craved unbiased information. Fortunately, our solicitor's secretary provided us with the name of a reputable criminal defense attorney. He was a godsend, as he calmly taught us the rudimentary basics of the legal processes concerning homicide. Reluctantly, we accepted that our contributions would be restricted by court procedure. Symbolically, we could stand in for our son, as he was not able to do so himself.

Through photos, letters of commendation, and tribute, we carried Liam directly to the faces and hearts of the authorities when we met with them. Personalizing Liam—a man who loved, and was loved in return—allowed us to feel less helpless.

∞

Important occasions drew near: Liam's birthday, then Christmas, both beyond our scope. Rallying for his birthday gave us an immediate purpose. We welcomed Liam's nearest and dearest to a local pub where, in happy times, the buddies had mustered for pool and darts. We chose to present gifts to them: copies of Liam's cottage sketch, his pool cue, one of his cameras, a signature jacket, and such. It had only been a month and a half since our son had been killed, and we held tight to denial and shock. Through stories and shared memories, his friends elevated Liam's birthday to a special night.

Within weeks, circumstances pushed us to care for Liam's century duplex and look out for his tenant. It tore at my heart. It felt too early to disturb his things; he could want to come home. However, with winter fast approaching, cold reality dictated that plans needed to be in place.

Sorting through Liam's home, his pride and joy, we braved a day steeped in unthinkable, throbbing torment. Furiously, I harangued the universe for its unseeing heartlessness. After a day so punishing, we dreaded the approaching darkness, but in time we succumbed to an exhausted and unsettled sleep.

Early next morning, there we were—full stop in the local hotel's quiet breakfast bar—bewilderedly gaping at the *Toronto Star's* open Sports section. Bold headlines shouted "Saint Liam Saves the Day, Rare Breed, Favoured to Win and Delivers." Saint Liam had come first in the Breeders' Cup Thoroughbred Race, the jockey resplendent in our Liam's favourite colours. The name, the colours, the timing—was it coincidence, a gift, or a sign? Never mind. We nestled into the comfort of this win—hugging tight to what seemed to us a heavenly message that Liam had arrived safe and sound. During our terrifying days and nights this solace was a pearl beyond price.

On a continuing basis, the distance to and from Stratford would prove daunting—two hours one way for us, more than six for Liam's dad. Eventually, Liam's lovely home would be sold, but there were more demons to stare down before then.

∞

"Like an ant on a stick, both ends of which are burning, I go to and fro without knowing what to do and in great despair ... Graciously look upon me. Thy love is my refuge." —Traditional prayer, India

Dreadfully unwell, I struggled to glimpse a shimmer of hope. Our friend Bevy sussed out a recommended grief therapist,[1] interviewing her extensively by phone. Amazing! By chance, the therapist's name was Beverley, the same as our friend. We were told that she

1 Years later, this same therapist would generously contribute Chapter Five, *Russell's Story*, to this book.

was a bereaved parent too. Nonetheless, we remained unconvinced as to the use of going. Without miraculously bringing back Liam, how could anyone lighten this darkness?

Following a brutal and unforgiving first Christmas of turning on each other, we needed to try something. We had lost far too much to lose each other as well. Wisely, our friend Roger questioned, "Why would you travel to a foreign country without a map?" His logic weakened our resolve. We phoned for an appointment.

Three months into our journey, January 2006, heralded a season of reaching out: therapy, yoga, grief seminars and drop-in support groups, books on bereavement, journaling, and portraiture of Liam. Urgently, we fought to understand the enemy—this spectre of grief, firmly entrenched in our midst.

Our therapist gave us a safe haven. We could be ourselves without masks, sharing anguish with no holds barred. She encouraged us to give voice to our anger, validating these wild extremes as a natural part of the grieving process. Gently but firmly, she insisted, "No matter what the courts decide, Liam is not coming back." It was hard to accept this dark truth.

∞

The year limped forward, legal processes grinding in ways mysterious to us. First there would be a pre-trial, with an Ontario Superior Court judge presiding. Most likely, this would happen in mid- to late summer.

As information was meted out during our meetings with the Crown, I alternately shielded my eyes then my ears. Cautiously and fearfully I strained to absorb the circumstances of Liam's shocking death—he should have been, could have been saved! There were witnesses, including a taxicab driver who had yelled out for those men to leave our son alone. The cabbie thought they would give up and take off. He called his dispatch not once but twice. While the OPP assured us that the police had come quickly, in our hearts we feared they had let Liam down.

"Before you embark on a journey of revenge, dig two graves." —Confucius

Rage, remorse, and dread!

Yearning to hurt those killers exactly as they had hurt Liam, it became a daily battle to tamp down my desire to lash out. This anger, which turned inward, also became a self-destructive force. I did not save my son; what kind of a mother was I? In therapy, we absorbed that grief is not logical; in yoga, we were shown that forgiveness of self and others is a continuing path. But oh, the shards of pain, the pits of ragged despair...

∞

The timing of the pre-trial, which had initially felt interminable, arrived too fast for our fragile states of mind. For months, we had dreaded July, stomachs roiling in anxiety. Now, here we were in this chilled courtroom. And with those men listening behind glass partitions, unwillingly we bore witness to the defense attorneys' dispassionate excuses for their clients' brutal, inexcusable actions. A travesty!

The law mandates that defense attorneys defend the accused; still, must we endure their disrespect? It felt as if our son was on trial. I wondered if it were possible, in this frigid courtroom, for me to combust, internally, into a fireball of blinding fury and pain. Our family and friends stood strong and tall while I fled the proceedings for fleeting reprieves. Once outside, I could seek refuge on a secluded patch of grass. Instinctively I hugged myself tight. Robotically rocking back and forth would soothe me for a moment or two, until my compulsive wringing of hands would begin again. Traumatized and fearful, I ached for my panic to subside—I prayed the searing summer heat would scorch away this stark cold dread.

Throughout this months-long process, with the ongoing help of friends and family, we "managed" through to the sickening end. For now, one step at a time was more than enough. It came to pass that there would be no jury trial; the judge alone would rule. Even this would take time. We were apprehensive that the Crown and defense attorneys would "join" (agree together on sentencing), leaving our impact statements, to be given prior to the sentencing, less sway with the judge. Though the Crown remained respectful of our back-and-forth input, we sensed our impotence.

The Crown and Defense did not join—instead they plea-bargained to lesser charges. In our opinions, these were miserably inadequate: manslaughter for one, aggravated assault for the other. How was a charge of aggravated assault even possible when this attack resulted in Liam's death?

Is it feasible the Crown attorneys did everything they could do, within the constraints they had? Perhaps this is so. Despite my despair, in objective moments I recognized them as decent men employed in a complex adversarial arena. And I reminded myself that the Crown prosecutes on behalf of the government, not on behalf of us or Liam. Just the same, the plea bargains left us feeling incensed and betrayed—the men furious, the women fighting tears.

By now, we had completed step one—a difficult step one. Court would continue in late summer or early fall. On our drive back home, the lyrics of Cher's iconic "If I Could Turn Back Time" gripped me in a new and different way. Given the chance, I would do this in a heartbeat.

∞

Court resumed in September, with fourteen impact statements presented to the Superior Court Judge—the accused, the lawyers, and all of us in attendance. So many spoke of how Liam's murder had impacted their lives. Surprisingly, we were advised the Orillia courtroom belonged to us. Never before had they received so many impact statements. In late afternoon on this emotion-packed day, we waited anxiously for a ruling—only to be told the sentencing would be delayed. The judge needed extra time to give due consideration to our statements. Although this delay made sense, the build-up left me sick to my stomach and weak in my knees—now there would be one more go-around.

As we faced the stress of another pending court attendance, our therapist urged us toward an eight-week support group with Bereaved Families of Ontario-York Region (BFOYR).[2] Sessions would begin in October. We resisted, worried that, immersed in our own desolation, it would prove insufferable to hear another's pain. However, with her continuing encouragement we agreed to try. This group blossomed into a precious gift. As we shared solace and stories with other parents, autumn sped along and our final court date loomed ominously.

2   BFOYR, a volunteer-based Ontario organization, provides valuable bereavement support locally. Hospice groups (available in many provinces and countries) also offer beneficial resources. The Compassionate Friends, a peer-based bereavement association founded in England in 1969, has grown beyond the UK, with sister groups in Australia, South Africa, many European countries, certain locales in Canada, and throughout the USA. Check with your health care provider for services accessible and helpful to you.

Then, regardless of the big build-up, suddenly it was over. Sandwiched between two cruel dates—the first anniversary of Liam's death and the second birthday (following his death)—the accused men were convicted and sentenced. They were given terms pitifully short for the magnitude of their actions and the enormity of Liam's loss, and ours.

Clustered on the courthouse steps, shivering in the brisk fall air, we reeled. Local reporters approached. "Excuse me, what do you think of the verdicts?" "Do you feel that justice has been served?" How is a parent to respond? What is the price for your child's life?

> *"Each of us is one of a kind. As ripples of grief surge outward—swelling to tremendous waves as they go, their effect reaches further than we can ever see, or ever know."* —Gwendolyn

Gratitude was not a familiar emotion for me then. Much later I could appreciate that the Crown, and the OPP Homicide Unit, must have pushed very hard indeed, to get this case to court so quickly. In the end, we were spared the possibility of many helpless years encased in numbing uncertainty.

∞

Liam, the boy, was a sunny bundle of mischief, running before he could walk, leaping into deep waters with abandon before he could swim. At the fearless age of three, our tyke remained blasé toward the grandeur of the Grand Canyon, chirping, "Mommy, I could climb that."

As he grew, sports came easily to him: ice skating, in-line blades, swimming, the skill (and nerve) to ski "the face" or slalom the biggest rooster tail from the back of a speed boat. Liam embraced it all. Inheriting a natural ear for music, with his dad's encouragement he taught himself the guitar, beginning as a baby when he tested out first steps, a toy replica in hand.

It felt as if Liam embraced friendships with those he sensed could use more kindness, extra attention. Recently, I read we relinquish most easily that which we have the most of. I pray this is true. An image of my son so secure he was cherished that he had extra love to spare and share sustains me in the dead of night when little else does.

Most humans have failings and Liam was no exception, yet he was the sort of man who would pull to the side of the road to rescue an injured pigeon. Was he too cavalier with the fragility of his own existence? I cannot know the answer, but I do know, absolutely, he did not deserve to die, and we did not deserve to lose him.

Today, consolation that Liam is remembered by others helps us. When we spot a Tim Horton's coffee at his grave, we see Bruce has shared a double/double and a chat. When the floral arrangements are pretty and fresh, we recognize Susan's touch as she changes seasons for Liam. Brent and Andrea named their third child for their friend, and Diane's girls asked for copies of Liam's portrait and cottage sketch as keepsakes. Our dear Jackie, when not holding my hands over tears and wine, sought out the places where her long-time friend had lived, each and every one, to sense his presence and to say goodbye.

"I miss him too," a neighbour declared, confiding that Liam had helped him with his countless bits and pieces of computer paraphernalia, patiently explaining which parts were worth keeping and why. Yes, there is much we did not know.

∞

Our therapist persistently inquired, "Will you have an unveiling?" Liam's headstone was ready to install. Although it was unfamiliar to us, we adopted this meaningful Jewish tradition, assembling a second graveside service. Friends and family participated in full, taking another chance to publicly mourn.

For the occasion, Liam's friends stepped up. Ian mastered "Amazing Grace" on his guitar in a mere two days, accompanying Shawna's flawless vocal rendition. Brent read the poem "The Measure of a Man." Friends and family all participated—each in their individual ways. By means of this warm-hearted support we borrowed courage. Just the same, within weeks, grief crashed upon us as a palpable force. The past year, while we had trusted we were facing our loss head on—really, we survived in suspended animation, waiting, waiting …

Regrettably, the distress of a lifetime spied an opening and moved right in.

Some counsellors suggest that grief may be cumulative. We had suffered an abundance of losses over the years—now, here they all were. Overshadowing this multitude were the untimely deaths of our cherished parents—and tight beside them the tragic passing of our precious young daughter-in-law (from a rare undiagnosed heart disease) a few brief years ago. Suddenly, each loss was unique, fresh, and too raw. On the heels of this sadness stormed in one of my deepest sorrows—finally, my fevered brain was persuaded it had the true and only answer. I was guilty. I was being punished.

You see, as a teenager, I had relinquished my newborn daughter to adoption. My baby's father asserted that we were far too young to be parents. He planned to finish university; he was not ready, nor willing, to marry just yet. University, at one time a hope, no longer was an option for me. I clung to my clerical position at Bell Canada.

Frightened for the future, I looked for support from close girlfriends. Then, before my courage failed me, I sought an interview with the Children's Aid Society—later, with a home for unwed mothers. The social workers and Anglican Church nuns were compassionate, though their main focus was the welfare and best interests of my unborn child. Childless couples of the 1960s were desperate to adopt infants, and the social mores of that day uniformly espoused a constrained judgement: a child needed two parents.

With two small brothers at home—the youngest not yet three years of age—I felt protective of my parents. While Dad worked every hour God gave, our young mother had her hands full running the household, caring for the family. As the firstborn, I bore a strong sense of responsibility for my actions.

In spite of my fears and uncertainties, planning ahead and finding options became essential. Discreetly, I approached the floor manager at my place of employment. He responded helpfully, promising to hold my job, with a guarantee of three months' unpaid leave. Honouring my request for privacy, a father himself, he expressed his concern, "Are you sure of your decision?" No, I was totally unsure, but this was not my response. What possible use could there be in sharing my uncertainties with a stranger, no matter how kindly his intent?

At this point, I worried constantly. Even so, the logistics I handled with ease—leading my family to believe I had a temporary job transfer to Sudbury. A sense of unreality masked the gravity of these arrangements. I was, after all, very nearly a child myself.

Unfitted shift dresses and looser clothing were popular then. Current fashions helped conceal my pregnancy from family as well as office colleagues. By the end of March, I entered into hiding in a home for unwed mothers. My beautiful girl was born on Mother's Day. Once the baby arrived, I was determined to keep her. For seven days in the hospital, holding her tight, I promised she would be safe. By this time, I could not stop sobbing. Right through the phone lines, Mom's x-ray vision exposed past deceptions. She implored, "We'll tell your father. He's sure to agree. Marry, and the three of you can live here at home." Mom promised to babysit while I returned to work, my baby's father to university.

"No," his answer was no!

Perhaps he was too fearful of his parents' disapproval. Or he could not face two more years of university, squashed and penniless, under my parents' watchful eyes—no matter how benign their gazes. I remained inconsolable, but he would not be swayed.

As an unwed mother, while undaunted by what strangers might think, painfully I considered, "What about my girl? What about taunts at school; what about bullying?" My early childhood had been charmed. Anchored by the stability of two loving parents, living in the same small village throughout the school years, I was blessed with friendships that continue to this day. I dreamt of this same security for her.

After the required six weeks, fearful of trapping my child in limbo, I signed the final adoption papers. With a profound and penetrating sadness, I catapulted into adulthood. In the face of these life-altering decisions—right or wrong—I chose not to burden my dad, although I suspect the weight of this secrecy was heavy for my mom to bear. As for me, any traces of the confident girl of childhood were scattered—dispersed and blown away by my own choices.

"So far as the east is from the west, so far has He removed our transgressions from us." —Psalm 103:12

Notwithstanding my initial certainty that I was being punished, in the Bible you will find more verses for forgiveness than for blame. Whatever your beliefs, I accept as truth that no God would punish the child for a parent's transgressions. Long ago we were forgiven. It is now time to forgive ourselves.

∞

By the year Liam was born, we had married. No one could take this child, not this time. He was six weeks premature, weighing a mere four-and-a-half pounds; I loved him with a fierce, protective passion. Three weeks following his birth, stabilized at five pounds, he was home in time for Christmas. While joyful that my boy was safe, there persisted within me a bottomless ache. My arms felt only half full. Liam's sister would be a two-and-a-half-year-old toddler, likely raising havoc, so excited for Santa to come. This pain had no chance for resolution; it was all too late.

Throughout Liam's childhood years, I could not forget his sister—was she happy, was she safe? Phone calls to the agency offered me little piece of mind. Given the privacy laws surrounding adoption, their responses, although polite enough, were generic at best. I harboured a secret continuing unease.

Amazingly, once my daughter turned nineteen, we found each other. Finally, with my own eyes, I could see that she was treasured. Coralie's parents, similar ages to my own mom and dad, had given her many advantages—most importantly, love and stability. Grief took a back seat, regrets not so much.

Following this emotional reunion, I garnered my courage and confessed to my dad about his granddaughter. Holding his head in his hands, he cried, "I let you down."

"My poor father, how could you let me down when you did not know?" Perhaps he is the richest example of the heavy mantle of parenthood, the quicksand of grief.

Years later, in deepest shock, Coralie attended her brother's funeral, confiding that, long ago, when I had cautioned her, "We are not always given time," she did not take this in. Perhaps, as many of us, Coralie had trusted that, within life's boundless stores of time, there would be uncountable chances for a relationship with her brother.

Before Liam left the cottage on that fateful October night, he had plucked me off my feet and swung me around the deck, declaring, "Love you, Mom."

"Liam, I love you too, but watch your back."

As I chased his black truck down our dark driveway—sensing a foreboding I could not identify—I shouted out for Liam to stop. He did not hear me. Despite this disquieting omen, I too trusted we had time.

∞

In December 2006, a few weeks after the sentencing, we regained the fortitude to register with Corrections Canada, so that we would be contacted in case either of the convicted men sought an early parole. Although it was intimidating, we deemed it vital to be aware and participate. With everything we could think to do for Liam done, our busyness halted. It felt as if we had been here before, after the courts, after the unveiling. But no, this time was different. Any fleeting remnants of shock and denial dissolved. Crash … we both crashed!

Even with the nurturing support we had received, our limited reserves were wiped out. They were used up by an unavoidably harsh exposure to the criminal justice system, in conjunction with the open wound of Liam's murder. All in all, I felt less like a whole person than an empty shell—a hollowed-out husk.

Thus, 2007 opened the floodgates to grieving and mourning. The life-saving grace was continuing in therapy, which afforded us a protected place to vent despair—a safe haven to talk when others could listen no more. We continued with drop-in groups, child-loss seminars, and yoga. Finding and consuming every grief book available gave me comfort. Absorbing how other parents coped lent us hope. Although each positive action helped, we uncovered no elixir.

While I read voraciously, Erwin was content to be nurtured second-hand with shared words and paragraphs. My next big choice was to choose to live. This may seem a natural, obvious resolve, but life events can erect imposing barriers to living with your pain and enduring your regrets. Fortunately for us, the scales were tipped in a positive direction by the (mutual) concern for family and the presence of close friends. Even so, we were living without colour, without flavour, sleep-walking through our days.

∞

Twenty-seven months after Liam's death, concerned friends and family nudged me. "Gwen, you have more to your life besides your son; you have a career, varied interests—including sports and travel. You have a big family, you have Erwin." Granting that this was true enough, innocently they had neglected to remember that Erwin—my love, my rock, and Liam's stepdad for more than twenty-three years—was walking a grief path too, on his own personal journey. In any case, all of this was beside the point. Before

Liam was murdered, certain trappings gave me surface fulfillment. After his death, this flimsy house of cards tumbled down.

> *"When the bough breaks, the cradle will fall, and down will come baby, cradle and all."* —*Mother Goose's Melody Book, first in print 1765*

Many interwoven hopes and dreams vanish when a child dies. Though Liam had enjoyed enduring relationships, he had not married—now he never would. He would not have children, no future chances to mature in stature or relish the fruits of his labour. There would be no long, happy life—everything had been wilfully and brutally stolen. While your child is alive, you might not comprehend how deeply your dreams are entangled with their lives. Our children are the future. Each one is matchless, holding a small essence of us. As the cradle, I felt that I did not protect the child.

"What is it about? What on earth is the point?" I could not figure it out.

During an evening child-loss seminar, a hypothetical scenario was posed by the speaker: "If grief is the cost of love and you could avert all of this pain by not having had your child in your life, what you would choose?" The question felt deceptively complex. Still, if those were my only two choices, I would be forced to pick the pain.

What about you?

I believe the point of grief is love, and these powerful, conjoined passions share an unbreakable bond. Although we were, to some degree, soothed by these irrefutable truths, our existence bore little resemblance to "living." With a deep-seated need for meaning and direction, in 2008 I sought facilitator training.

Early on I recognized that mentoring bereaved parents, while conveying validation to them, could introduce hope to our lives too. The groups are self-help based, and volunteering continued to nurture a sense of purpose in me.

Then, within a short space of time, the following two seemingly unrelated incidents occurred—one hurtful, one hopeful …

Sadly, shame and anger can accompany the trauma and grief of homicide, especially when surviving victims are exposed to insensitive speculations and inappropriate questions, such as "What was he doing there at that time of night? Was he dealing in drugs?"

"No! No! Unequivocally, no—my Lord, how can you even ask this awful thing?" Do you think that blaming a helpless victim for his own death somehow ensures that your child will stay safer?

The sad fact is, many of us struggle with awareness and empathy—it is helpful to remember the words we choose hold power to either harm or comfort. In the face of my ongoing pain, fuelled by the hurtful misunderstandings of strangers, I pondered … Was there something else I could do that might soften the path for other surviving victims of homicide?

Later this same year, Christine, Services Coordinator at BFOYR, asked if I would write a paper about how grief is impacted by the court system. Although I was intrigued, my self-confidence was sorely lacking. I had to think further. Graphically, I relived the sessions at court and my terror of further injustices to Liam. Recalling the heedless barbs of strangers and my fervent mission to defend Liam's memory, it was as if an all-consuming fire scorched my heart. With Christine's request flooding my mind, an irresistible urge surfaced: to reach out to a surviving victim, the one who could be me.

Inhibited by self-doubt, I stalled. "I cannot visualize how to begin."

But a tenacious inner voice propelled me forward: "You need to do this!"

Slowly galvanized, I became not only engaged but *driven*. Benefiting from a rich abundance of helping hands and wise counsel, by the third anniversary of my son's death this requested paper expanded into *Grief and the Courts*, a not-for-profit booklet dedicated to Liam's memory.

Scarcely had Erwin assured me that our efforts would be worthwhile when the booklet was whole-heartedly adopted by the Ontario Victim Services Secretariat (OVSS).[3] Hard copies became widely accessible to surviving victims. We felt disbelief and gratitude in equal measure. Then, generously, a manager from one of the OVSS offices nominated me for the Attorney General's Victim of Distinction Award. In 2010, accompanied by other recipients, I received this recognition. Shortly afterward, the booklet was introduced online in both English and French.

Though I was heartened by this success and honoured by the award, it became perversely complicated for me to separate thoughts of Liam's murder from these accolades. While I spiralled downward, a mentor counselled, "When you least expect it, the power of grief can bring you to your knees. Please remember, you stood up before; you will stand again. As hard as it feels, it is about choices."

"It does not matter how slow you go, as long as you do not stop." —*Confucius*

∞

A time of reflection ensued for me. Reviewing life choices, mine and Liam's, found me back in 1998. My son's move to Stratford

---

3   OVSS, under the Ministry of Ontario's Attorney General, works to ensure that victims of crime are treated with respect and receive the information they need.

was an enormous task, onerous for just the two of us. Erwin was on assignment in England and everyone else was busy. Fortunately, Liam's friends Brent and Andrea were at the other end to help unload and unpack—furniture in place, tick, kitchen cupboards stocked, tick, waterbed filled, tick, pictures hung, tick, pizza and beer for four, tick, tick. Liam's temporary rental glowed cozily, awaiting his return, as we locked up tight.

After slogging away the whole long day, we returned the leased truck well past midnight. Since he was too tired for the return drive to Stratford, Liam would spend this night at home. Physically and emotionally spent, with the reality of his new job imminent, Liam began to second-guess the wisdom of taking this out-of-town I.T. position. I worried that it was my fault. Perhaps I shouldn't have encouraged him to go for it, to give change a chance!

When I voiced my concerns, Liam jumped in, "Mom, don't you know you are my hero? I want to make you proud of me." Nearly mute with fatigue, I assured him that I already was proud of him but, most of all, wanted him to stay true to himself. Could I have said more? No matter the child's age—because ever and always my child, he was very much a grown man—it can be an ongoing struggle, as a parent, to let yourself off the hook for saying too much, or alternatively saying too little.

During this journey, I have found that mentally reliving our lives, striving to make sense of it all, delicately unpicking the threads, are normal elements of grief work. Whenever I falter, an echo of Liam's big-hearted words spurs me to try harder. However flawed a hero I may be, I cannot give up if this is what he thinks.

∞

Through BFOYR my reaching-out continued. While facilitating a child-loss group, I assigned homework to all the moms and dads: Write a letter to your child …

Dear Liam,

This coming Sunday is your birthday, the sixth one since your death. In our lives, we have taken too much for granted—never fearing such brutality could happen to you. There have been days, lately, when it is easier to suspend belief than to face the reality of your murder. Living through this: a parent's worst nightmare, has taken more courage than we knew we had.

Do you recognize the African proverb that proclaims, "It takes a village to raise a child"? We have learned it takes that same village (and more so) to rise up and rescue the parents if the child dies. Thankfully, we have this community, warmly embracing, wrapping us in their collective arms. Liam, some of its residents, and our helpmates, are your dear friends.

Can I ask, just once more, why in heaven's name you stopped at that place—putting yourself at such dire risk? It is hard to stay away from those dark roads—especially seductive on the anniversaries of your birth and death—when I agonize that, alone and afraid, you were calling out for me before you died.

While we strive to let go of anger, guilt, and hopelessness, it becomes impossible to pick the most ruthless one, since each has stretched the very heart and soul of us. Only with persistent grief work have we come to know that anger, revenge, and fear hold no light, no hope. We stay truer to all we love by reaching for the good that remains.

Selling your century home battered our hearts. Revisiting the repairs you completed, some with Erwin's help and some with your dad's, was beyond poignant. Remember on that final cottage weekend, you arrived a day late because you delayed at home to hang shelves? Good job! Your house looked great, selling for what you expected had you decided to sell. I confess that our efforts to side-step a quagmire of regret have been fruitless. This worldly success and profit belongs to you, not us.

The police, the courts, the lawyers! We did our best, since you could not do so for yourself. Friends and family rallied, letting one and all know how much they cared. You have made a difference, Liam, and we are proud of you. Then again, you know this …

One September morning, when, with nervous trepidation, we visited a gifted psychic medium, you came through loud and clear. Even with our scepticism, it was tough to deny your presence. Surprising confidences were revealed to us—confidences only you and we knew. Ah well, it seems you are busy and happy. While treasuring this uplifting image, my love, we miss you still.

- Over the years, writing, reading hopeful narratives, studying, and mentoring—mingled with a boost from sports and the optimism of nature—have lifted me.
- Trying to answer the hard questions while asking them of myself too has been significant in seeking insight.
- Out of the blue, a cousin wondered, "Gwen, you are living with two vast losses; which is the worst one?" Unquestionably, Liam's murder is the worst—both are to do with separation and loss, but here the similarity ends. One is life, the other is death.
- Kahlil Gibran speaks it best with his gentle poetry. I too believe that we do not own our children. They own their lives. My prayers and hopes are for their happiness and safety. It is not about me, it is about them …

Whereas my stepchildren have not been spared life's adversities or its most penetrating sorrows, at the moment they are healthy—doing their best to stay happy. My dear Coralie is safe, and insofar as the human condition allows it, I believe she is content. Accordingly, while regret hovers, I am reassured. The senseless waste of Liam's violent death remains my life-hurdle; equally I hold a prayer that he too is safe.

Some nights, before I sleep, I must battle the voices—the ones that insist on guilt, persist in blame. My friend Maureen calls them The Committee. In Sanskrit they are known as Vrittis.[4] My delightful late mother proclaimed this intrusive head racket to be the devil on your shoulder, heckling in your ear. In her wisdom and humour, she warned me, "Don't pay attention to that nonsense." By whatever title you know them, they can be relentless and mean. At the day's end, I reach for something hopeful to read—turning, in time, to meditation and prayer. Eventually, The Committee packs up and slinks away ... good riddance.

Walking in my changed world, I rediscover meaning when I give back—choosing kindness instead of judgement, forgiveness rather than blame. Erwin grounds me, reiterating, "We only can do our best with what we know at the time; hindsight does not count." Family and friends sustain us, eager to toss a life ring if need be. Just the other evening, like-minded confidants joined us for dinner. It was such good fun. On the dance floor, I actually laughed out loud.

Although grief does not stray too far, recognizing its devious face, we visit for a little while, and I no longer fear this misery will never leave. In this different place, at this new time, in keeping with sorrow there is love. Though I respect my sadness, I welcome hope—shining on the horizon like a brilliant rainbow.

---

4   **Vrittis**: literally, "whirlpool," waves or ripples of disturbance

With each of our children clasped tight to my heart, Liam's loss remains my ever-tender ache. Still and all, with the kinship of family and the support of cherished friends, we have an abundance of blessings. Do not lose sight of hope. I believe that we who remain are here for a significant reason.

> *"With all its sham, drudgery, and broken dreams, it is still*
> *a beautiful world. Be cheerful. Strive to be happy."*
> —Desiderata, Max Ehrmann

Please hold on to this: "As hard as it feels, it is about choices." If we choose to, we can ski the lofty peaks.

Chapter Two

Alan's Story

Carol Reid-LeClair

Alan Clayton Reid:
June 4, 1976–December 6, 2005

"Memories of love abound
In my heart and in my mind
They give me comfort, keep me sane
And lift my spirits up again."
—Anonymous

Alan's Story

On December 6, 2005, my husband, Bill, and I were in St. Pete's Beach for a two-week holiday, scheduled to return home for Christmas. We had been in Florida just a few days when, following a day of Christmas shopping, we arrived back at our motel to a message from the police, asking us to call as soon as possible.

Perplexed, we wondered if perhaps our house had been burglarized while we were away. At 6:45 p.m. Bill called the police officer. After a brief conversation, we were told that my son Alan, only twenty-nine years old, had committed suicide. Motionless, helpless, I was frozen in the middle of the room—gripped with shock, despair, and in complete bewilderment.

Dead—how could he be dead?

We had talked just a few days earlier. I had reminded Alan that when we returned from Florida all of us would celebrate a happy Christmas Day together. What on earth had happened?

My mind refused to take in this horrific information.

My son had been under the care of a psychiatrist. Alan was taking medication to alleviate the symptoms of mental illness he had been struggling with for the previous two years. Of course, I worried, and often questioned, "How are you doing, truly?" Usually his answer was brief, but inevitably he would assure me that, actually, he was okay. I trusted him, and had faith the psychiatrist was helping him cope with this disease.

Bombarded with intense emotions, with which I did not know how to cope, first I needed to call my daughter, Christine, back home. It was essential to ask her to get in touch with family members and tell them about her brother.

We would be flying home to Ontario as soon as we could get a flight. Then what?

Speaking with the coroner that evening, I repeated the same question over and over: "What do I do now?" The coroner was patient with me. He explained that Alan was in the morgue. We needed to contact a funeral parlour, and they would make the arrangements to pick him up. But I could not remember these instructions, so finally I wrote everything down. In shock, I was not processing what was said to me.

Returning home was a bewildering blur. Vaguely, I remember being on a plane. All of my focus was on my son's death; unable to grasp how to manage the next few hours and days, I had no room to contemplate the coming weeks, months, or years.

Although I was overcome with anguish and disbelief, it was crucial to find a way to function. There was so much to do … As soon as we arrived home, I contacted a funeral parlour. They assured me they would take care of Alan and guide us through the process. In hindsight, I must say the funeral parlour we chose was helpful and compassionate throughout this time of inconceivable panic and grief.

Finally, the arrangements were in place, and family and friends had been notified. Some were contacted several times, because I would forget who had been called. Fortunately, my daughter arrived the night we returned. It was uplifting just to see her face; her love and support were a godsend. Nevertheless, each of us was deeply mired in a cruel, unending nightmare from which we could not wake.

Christine wanted to compile a photo-collage of her brother with his family and his friends, to be displayed at the funeral. With our emotions still raw, we leafed through family photo albums—choosing favourite pictures from past events and happy times, evoking the talented, caring man we knew. Pulled back in time, I reminisced with my lovely girl about the day I first laid eyes on her big brother. My mind flooded with memories …

∞

Naturally, as my firstborn, he was the most beautiful baby I had ever seen. We had an instant attachment from the moment the nurse placed Alan in my arms. As if it was yesterday, I recalled that he looked up at me, blinked, and stopped crying. He snuggled in and was content as long as I was holding him. Overwhelmed with tenderness for my newborn child, I vowed to protect him forever. Our connection was apparent to everyone around us. When my mother-in-law, Jean, first saw her grandson with me, she exclaimed that she could feel the bond. "Pure love," she whispered, with a smile. I felt blessed.

Once Alan could crawl, many times he would wrap his arms and legs around one of my ankles, giggling, while I laboured around the house with him hanging on. He delighted in this mischievous capture of Mommy. My heart was full.

As a youngster, he was so focused on storybooks that I loved reading to him. With his enthusiastic curiosity, it became a treat to walk to the park, passing time on the swings and slides. Alan gleefully embraced the simple delights in life: picking flowers, blowing dandelion-fluff to the wind and soap-bubbles to the sky.

For him it was magic—watching the fluff float free, the bubbles burst into rainbows.

By the time his baby sister arrived, Alan was two-and-a-half years old. He was totally mesmerized by her in the beginning, but after only six weeks he asked me to send her back. The novelty had worn off. His father and I laughed, and assured him that Christine was here to stay. Of course, as most siblings do, they loved each other, had their squabbles, and moved on.

∞

Alan was a happy child. When he attended daycare, his teachers shared anecdotes of how he would be the first to start laughing at a funny book or an amusing movie; before long, his teachers and the other children would be chuckling too. Alan had a contagious, carefree laugh and a beautiful smile. I loved his smile. He was a sensitive, kind, smart little boy.

Adoring the water, he participated in swimming lessons from the time he was a baby. Alan was a quick study, advancing quickly to the level of "Maroon" with confident ease. Still, I picture him leaping into the pool, so excited to start his lesson, swimming through the water like a fish. We enjoyed many lighthearted after-noons jumping in and out of my parents' pool.

At only five years old, when his aunt purchased her first computer, my son was hooked. He embraced technology, never looking back. Visiting his aunt often, he sat at her computer for hours with a thirst to learn as much as he could. By the time Alan was ten, he had an old Commodore 64. Even then, he started inputting programs that he had created.

Yes, there was outdoor fun too; we would drive to the country with the kids, find a stream, and fish the day away. Christine and Alan looked forward to our summer escapades. During one outing, Alan caught a twenty-six-inch fish—so exciting for him and for his little sister too.

Christine was five-and-a-half years old, and her brother eight, when we scheduled a road trip down east. Eager for adventure, we were not disappointed. Never had we seen the ocean before, and it was thrilling. Wherever possible, Alan jumped over the waves as they crashed to the shore, laughing and welcoming the challenge. Meanwhile, our little girl scampered up the rocks, resolved to flee those very same waves, her blonde hair blowing wildly in the wind.

Continuing on to Prince Edward Island, we captured the sights and sounds of eastern Canada. One sunny morning, Alan's dad treated him to a fishing expedition while our daughter chose shopping. Christine's hazel eyes brightened with excitement as we explored for souvenirs to bring home. She selected a colourful beaded necklace, crafted by a local First Nation artisan, her face glowing with pleasure as I fastened it around her neck.

∞

Recollecting with Christine, my heart and mind were drawn to the ordinary times, the everyday safe stories ...

Alan liked school; he took his schoolwork seriously and excelled, making friends who stayed with him for years to come. He appeared to be well-adjusted as a child, an adolescent, and later as a young adult. Throughout the years, painstakingly I re-examined those younger days, endlessly searching for indicators that might foretell my son's mental illness. Quite simply, I could not find them. All I could see was Alan relishing his childhood as much as any other boy. Just the same, as parents will do, I berated myself, time and again—convinced that I must have missed the signs.

Of course life wasn't perfect. When Alan was ten years old, his little sister eight, they endured a divorce between their father and me, and I felt their pain along with my own. The kids would visit their dad every other weekend, while my heart ached for what they were going through. Eventually, as time passed, it became a routine situation and circumstances moved us forward. After four years on my own, I met and married Bill, a wonderful man who cherished Alan and Christine as if they were his own children. We adjusted, came together, and loved each other as a family.

For the most part, Alan breezed through high school. When he stumbled over a few bumps on his journey, his stepdad was there to guide him with helpful suggestions. Alan respected Bill, appreciating his help and the words of wisdom he offered.

∞

The summer Alan turned seventeen, I taught him to drive in my high-performance Mustang convertible. It makes me smile to recall how he absolutely loved driving this sporty car, on occasion impishly suggesting, "Come on, Mom, let me set it free?" Naturally, he already knew the answer to that one, sneaking a peek at me while we shared a little chuckle.

In December 1992, after passing his driver's test, Alan looked hard for a part-time job so he could purchase his first car. His father helped him locate a second-hand vehicle, and he was delighted. Often he would pick up a couple of friends on the way to class—all a part of enjoying his high school years.

Then, toward the end of grade twelve, Alan met and fell in love with a lovely young lady. They were inseparable. Incredibly, by the end of the school year, they had moved into their own place. Initially I was pretty upset. They were both so young that it felt hasty and premature to be this serious. Be that as it may, he was happy, eighteen years old, with the world at his feet.

Predictably, Alan found a position working with computers; he was a natural at solving problems and technical difficulties. Life was good for him and his girlfriend, living on their own terms and so much in love. There they were, at the various family gatherings—barbeques with Bill cooking steaks, birthday parties, Christmas celebrations, all the regular day-to-day events and the normal contented times.

After seven years as a couple, in May of 2002, Alan revealed that he was suffering from depression, and his girlfriend wanted to end their relationship. This news came as a big shock to me. Truly, I had not seen it coming. It had looked as if they were having a few issues, but I assumed they would work them out.

When I look back at this time in Alan's life, I realize this depression was the beginning of his mental illness. My son hid the gravity of his struggles from everyone. He did not want to worry us. And I had not grasped the seriousness of his disease.

Yes, sadly, I had missed a sign.

Still and all, not too long after his separation, Alan gave the impression he was back on his feet. Working at a different job, he was taking a break from the stress of repairing and setting up computers. Every Sunday afternoon he would stop by to spend time with Bill and me. Alan would bring along a special treat—usually Häagen-Dazs ice cream bars. We would relax, watch some TV—often Texas Hold'em poker—while we chatted. Appreciating each other's company, we looked forward to these weekly catch-up visits. It was comforting to see him doing this well, or so we thought ...

∞

While sorting through the family photos with my daughter—piecing together a collage of her brother's life—I felt a loss so profound that I could hardly breathe. Exactly how would I survive the death of my son? How could I possibly cope?

The next few days saw me in a daze, moving about in muted slow motion. Bits and pieces of memory surface, such as re-visiting the funeral parlour to complete last-minute arrangements. But so much remains surreal, with little solid substance. To the funeral director, I kept repeating that a parent should never have to bury a child. It is supposed to be the other way around. Life was sorely out of sync for me.

Alan's funeral presented a maze of people approaching to express their sympathies and condolences to me. Recognizing their faces, seeing their mouths moving, I could not decipher a word they were saying, so I just nodded and murmured, "Thank you for coming."

My stepdaughter, Krista, gave a eulogy of Alan's life, and I recall her at the podium speaking. Later, during the luncheon, I overheard admiring comments about what a beautiful job Krista had done in honouring Alan. Yet I was a step removed. Perhaps, for this one day, shock had allowed me to observe my life from a safer distance.

The funeral had taken place on December 10, two weeks before Christmas. My heart sank as the twenty-fifth approached. Christine returned to her home. Everyone else had moved on with their lives. It was a concept I could not fathom—move on? My life had been shattered, and Christmas was looming—a day where nostalgic yearnings for times past, alongside society's pervasive imagery of "perfectly happy families," would be inescapable for me. As I looked around me, celebrations were everywhere. The local mall was fully garbed in lights and garlands, with Christmas music constantly playing. The shoppers, happily drifting through the aisles, were enjoying the moment—something I could never imagine for myself not now. I refused to put up decorations; I could not participate in the festivities. It was physically hurtful to endure this joyful season, with my mind and heart bursting from the sadness of Alan's death.

Fortunately, the week prior to the twenty-fifth, my daughter convinced us to join her and her boyfriend for Christmas. After cooking a casserole, my husband and I travelled to Christine's apartment, an hour away. We spent the day together; foregoing a traditional turkey dinner seemed right to us all. This small choice changed the schematics just enough that we were able to get through. For the sake of my husband, my daughter, my step-daughter, and my whole family, whom I love, I tried to be present. All the same, I was relieved when the day finally ended. The pain of my son's death was indescribable. He needed to be there with us; his presence was greatly missed.

∞

Alan had been living at a friend's house, where he had his own room. Now we were obliged to deal with his possessions. Even the thought of doing so was devastating. Bill and I met with my son's friend, Chris, and Chris's wife; together we sorted through Alan's belongings.

As well, my son had left clothes and boxes at our home. Whenever I could manage, I looked through his things. It was a heart-wrenching task. As I came across special items, which I remembered Alan collecting, I gave them a place of prominent display. I was compelled to keep his memory alive; having his personal collection nearby, along with photos of him, brought me comfort.

In the weeks following Christmas, I moved through the motions of rising every morning. Encased in a heavy mental fog, I followed my schedule like a robot. I was automated. I was numb. Then, in early January, with a burning need to do something useful—anything that might divert my sorrow—I resolved to return to my office job. So back to work I went, even though it had been just a month since Alan's tragic death. No matter how hard I strained to channel my thoughts, I would sit at my desk aching from an overwhelming sadness—the same sadness that had blanketed me since our life-changing phone call.

Finally, after six months of striving to regain some normalcy, I chose to leave my job. My grief was taking over. I did not feel equal to the challenge of going to work every day, pretending that all was natural and routine in my world. Too often I drove to the office with tears streaming down my cheeks. Many times, in desperation, I longed to scream to an uncaring world, "My life isn't normal anymore. My son is dead." It was tough to witness co-workers, friends, family, and even strangers living their lives, seemingly safe and secure from the heartache that pulled at me twenty-four hours a day.

No longer working, I had much more time to think about my son—what had Alan been going through? Why, oh why, had he not confided in me that with his illness overtaking him, he sensed a compulsion to take his own life?

My mind continued to work overtime, and then the guilt set in. I became certain it was my fault my son had died. As his mother, I should have been able to save him. There must have been something I could have said or done that would have stopped him from taking this irreversible step. I felt helpless and filled to the brim with regret.

Yearning to talk about my son's life, and his death, I needed to speak with someone who could help me put my grief, and guilt, into some kind of perspective, but my family did not want to listen. Perhaps they were coping in their own ways. Everyone was moving forward with their lives except me. I could not; I did not want to.

At a certain point, a friend told me that she did not wish to hear anything more about my grief. Okay, no more talking with her. On top of this were the comments from family and friends that it was time to move on, a phrase I dislike to this day. In my experience, it is not possible to move on from the death of one's child. However, with help, it is possible to inch forward.

Throughout the years, my mother-in-law had been a source of great support for me. Although my marriage to her son had ended in divorce, Jean always offered a shoulder for me to lean on and gave freely with an open heart. After Alan's death, we would get together for an afternoon to share cups of tea, talk, and cry. We seemed able to relate to each other in our time of grief, and to disclose our feelings of helplessness. But as soothing and healing as these talks were, my broken heart demanded to speak with someone on a more objective level.

Searching in the local newspapers for the Bereaved Families of Ontario contact information I had spotted a few months earlier, this time I wrote the number down. For a week I struggled to dredge up the courage to call. On a particularly bad day, I phoned and left a message, inquiring if they had sessions for a parent who has lost a child. Within days, I received an answer; they had a group coming up in a few weeks. I asked for my name to go on that list. Urgently, I needed to open up about my grief from losing my son, with all of its painful feelings.

At my first session, I immediately liked the two facilitators leading the group. When they told their heartbreaking stories of losing their sons, I finally started to feel that I was not alone in my grief. In this group, one couple had lost their five-year-old daughter; another couple's young adult son had died in a tragic motorcycle crash; there was a mum whose adult daughter had recently died. As each one shared their painful stories, I became unsure when my turn came if I would be able to speak. It all was so sad.

Slowly, I started to explain that while my husband and I were in Florida, my son had committed suicide. The people in the group were really listening—truly understanding my pain. I continued to attend the sessions; I talked, and talked, and talked. It was definitely good therapy for me. Nonetheless, when the group ended, even though I felt somewhat stronger, grief and pain remained my daily companions.

∞

Some of the biggest obstacles, during the first year, were the anniversary dates; 2006 was bursting with painful firsts: Mother's Day, Alan's birthday, my birthday, family weddings, and the first anniversary of my son's shocking suicide.

On Mother's Day, Alan's absence was far too real. Habitually, he had made a big deal of the day, with a bouquet of red roses along with chocolate, but most of all a visit. My daughter now lived hours away, working on the weekends, diligently staying well-occupied. Her busy schedule was one of her coping mechanisms for missing her brother. Certainly, Christine sent a card, and we chatted on the phone while I attempted to focus on my mom—putting the emphasis on Mother's Day for her, not me. Even so, it remained a terrible day filled with sorrow.

As the year progressed, there was Alan's milestone birthday. He would have turned thirty years old, and it dragged me down with despair. He should be here celebrating; instead, we were mourning his death. Everywhere I went I spotted something that triggered memories—things Alan liked, items he would have collected. It was wrenching to get up and function each day.

During family gatherings, his absence pierced my heart. The weddings we attended for my nieces and nephews were especially rough. Although genuinely pleased for them and their shining futures, I remained remorseful—sad that Alan would never be married, have a family of his own, or a future.

∞

Looking back, I believe the first year I was still in shock, full of grief and denial, not knowing where to turn for help. As difficult as that year was, the second year was challenging in a different way. Painfully, with shock and disbelief behind me, the reality that my son was gone forever hit full force.

In this, my new normal, I was driven to research Alan's illness further. I needed to know as much as possible—anything at all that might shed light on my endless question: "Why?"

Following are a few of my findings about schizoaffective disorder (a mental illness that disables a person's ability to function and manage everyday tasks):

- One patient out of ten with this illness commits suicide.
- Generally, this is because medication is ineffective in keeping symptoms under control.
- My son heard voices; also, he suffered from paranoia and depression.
- Alan's medication would work for about six weeks and then the symptoms would return.

After two years, he gave up. In his suicide note, Alan said, "No one is to blame; I just can't live with this illness any longer." With compassion for myself and Alan, gently I replenished my understanding that my son had died because he was so very sick. He believed he would never get any better. Whenever I would plunge into darkness or descend into guilt, I reminded myself that Alan had been living, and struggling, with a debilitating disease—a disease, tragically, he was unable to conquer, no matter how hard he tried.

∞

During the second year, I craved doing something special in honour of Alan's life. I had heard that the town of Newmarket was planting trees, called Celebration of Life Trees, in remembrance of those who have died. A personalized plaque is positioned at the tree's base. Contacting the town, I inquired about having a tree planted in my son's memory. Feeling good about this idea, I went ahead and ordered one.

In the fall of 2007, Alan's tree was planted alongside a main path in Fairy Lake Park. Shortly afterward, my daughter met me there. She wanted to see the Celebration Tree for herself. Christine and I hugged as we read the plaque, admiring this verdant living symbol of her brother's life. Numerous times, my husband and I, my son's friends, and many family members have walked in Fairy Lake Park paying loving tribute to Alan.

My daughter struggled with the loss of her brother too, and we leaned on each other as much as possible. Around this time, Christine decided to enroll at Georgian College. She was trying to move forward. I supported her efforts to pursue her education while she took brave steps in putting her life, and hope, back together. This was not easy to do, but Christine is a powerhouse when she sets her mind on a goal. Working relentlessly, she successfully completed her three-year degree course, choosing a positive, healing path.

∞

A good friend of mine, whom I met at one of the Bereaved Families follow-up meetings, once told me, "One second, one minute, one hour, and one day at a time—this is how we move forward after such a devastating loss." I agree with her comment, which has helped me through many a difficult day.

While I think of my son every single day, now I dwell on the happier times: remembering our warm chats, spontaneous laughter, listening to his music with him—the twenty-nine years of "Alan moments." My focus has moved from how he died to how he lived, and I have photos around the house of him smiling back at me.

Every year, in December—a month that is especially difficult, as it was just before Christmas that Alan died—Bill and I join with BFOYR for the Memory Tree of Light gathering. We light a candle for Alan, acknowledging publically that he is treasured, remembered, and loved. This has become a meaningful and comforting tradition for us.

Naturally, it saddens me that my son is not here, especially when an exciting event happens or when I see something unusual. For instance, Alan would have delighted in the new technology we enjoy today. So much has changed in this field since his death. As an enthusiastic techie, computers enthralled Alan; he would have prized an iPhone even more. Every now and then it flashes across my mind to tell Alan about an amazing find before

I immediately recall that of course I cannot. Though an image of him with all these new toys makes me chuckle, these moments are poignant too. They vividly evoke what we have lost—bringing waves of sorrow, along with the uglies of grief: anger, guilt, and despair. Fortunately, this heavy melancholy does pass, letting me treasure what we had, allowing me to return to the love and hope that remain.

Life pulls us forward. I have learned how to move right along with it, striving to step out into the future with the friends and family members who are here in my life now, and who need me. I know my son would want this.

My days unfold with the love of my family, the smiles on my grandchildren's faces bringing joy into my world again. I cherish this. I believe that each and every one of us needs happiness and joy, don't you?

Yes, there is life after tragedy, "one second, one minute, one hour, and one day at a time."

This life-force that draws me forward draws my son forward too. Alan, who is lovingly remembered by his family and by his friends, will hold a cherished place in our hearts forever.

Truly, love and hope never die.

Chapter Three

Adrian's Story

Helen Jay

Adrian Gordon Jay:
June 11, 1976–September 20, 2002

*"Throughout our lives we are sent
precious souls ...
meant to share our journey,
however brief or lasting their stay
they remind us why we are here.*

To learn...to teach...to nurture...to love."
—*"Some People" by Flavia Weedn*

Adrian's Story

Painting Adrian:

Following are just a few reflections about our son:

An avid outdoorsman, he devoted his life to the personal development of others. His works, passions, and charismatic personality impacted all those he touched. Adrian had a truly beautiful spirit, and my unending respect. He wanted to be and was a leader.

He stood a man of good character—always I will remember him as bright, warm, and giving. He was an amazing person, yet humble. He had a way of making the most boring things seem to have a life of their own, and he did crazy things just for the hell of it. Adrian touched, inspired, and empowered many kids.

> *"Some People"*
> *They help us to see that everything on earth*
> *is a part of the incredibility of life …*
> *and that it is always there*
> *for us to take of its joy.*
> *—Flavia Weedn*

Months after his death, we were still receiving condolence letters from friends, family, casual acquaintances, the YMCA, and Scouts Canada. There were letters with stories and thoughts expressing high regard for a young man whose life ended much too soon, notes regarding Adrian's character, behaviour, and undertakings. It struck me over and again that, because of his travels, independent lifestyle, and unassuming way, there was much in the last few years of Adrian's life about which we were not completely aware. We did know, however, he had accomplished a great deal in his short time here on earth. Those accomplishments were well memorialized by those who valued him.

In Nova Scotia, a leadership building was erected by Scouts Canada in his memory. Four services were given for Adrian: one in northern Ontario; two in Halifax, Nova Scotia; and another in British Columbia. At the time, it was overwhelming. Although we sincerely treasured the honour for Adrian, for me there were moments in which these services exaggerated and underlined the depths of our loss.

"We all long for the knowledge that others cared for the deceased." —*Unknown*

We knew and loved our son deeply. We knew him as a youthful risk-taker, who on occasion could be impulsive. We knew him as kind, loving, funny, and very charming—despite his moments of impatience and stubbornness. In a room, he was a positive, strong presence. Yet Adrian was also shy and often unsure of himself. He was a human being who experienced uncertainties, joys, sorrows, failures, and successes. The world lost a great young man; all who loved him miss him.

"The meaning of the lives of the deceased is not cancelled by their deaths." —*Unknown*

There exists a handwritten list of things Adrian hoped to complete and experience—his early bucket list. I have much respect for his privacy; therefore, I will not disclose the entire list. But as I paint his spirit, I am comfortable sharing the following wishes:

- *Talk with a world leader*
- *Know the flow of many activities, including: thought, climbing, leadership, fly-fishing, and guitar*
- *Create a method for emotional self-rescue*
- *To be satisfied, but never content with my being*
- *To truly know someone else*
- *Know myself*
- *Sleep in a tent in a hurricane*
- *Make Thanksgiving dinner in the woods*
- *Justifiably kick someone's ass*
- *Work for a costumer, not as an employer*
- *Create a sculpture*
- *Meet a mentor*
- *Be a mentor*
- *Watch a birth*

Some of the goals on this list he did indeed achieve.

Painting Shock:

We raised and educated Adrian in Nova Scotia. The last conversation we had with him was during his drive from his Ontario residence to Halifax, where he was to be the emcee at his best friend's wedding. The young minister who married the lovely couple also performed the Celebration of Life ceremony for Adrian, the day after the wedding.

Just three hours from his destination, Adrian was involved in a serious car accident. At 2:00 on the morning of Sept 16, 2002, we received the call. Adrian's partner was on the telephone repeating a conversation she had just finished with two policemen, who had gently relayed sketchy information of that fatal event. We knew right away that if Adrian was not delivering this news, he was severely wounded. After a very blunt and crushing telephone conference with the treating neurologist, we understood, without a doubt, that our son was going to die, possibly within twenty-four hours. What was described concerning his countless injuries sickened us. He was in a deep coma, on life support.

An image I will never clear from memory is that of my husband, John, on his knees before me, telling me how very sorry he was. The numbness ... the horror ... the disbelief...the ache, is indescribable. This felt as if it couldn't be real. It had been only a little over a day ago that we all discussed spending time together upon his return. Life changed immediately and forever.

What our hearts could cope with was a very long time in catching up with what our minds knew. This was too sudden. There were no good-byes, no last hugs.

Automatically, we switched into task mode, not allowing emotions to take command; we just couldn't. Battling shock, we made several calls—the most difficult to Adrian's older brother, Anthony, who struggled desperately to grasp what he was hearing. At one point during those first few hours, Anthony seemed to reject the news entirely. Repeatedly, he asked, "How could this happen?" and "What exactly happened?" He was angry and disbelieving. We could not provide one single answer.

The memory of methodically packing for a funeral still astonishes me. We arranged an emergency flight out of Toronto—all of the family and Adrian's partner, seated together. I still wonder how we managed these tasks with such speed and accuracy. Nevertheless, in a few hours, there we were—row twenty-six—in tears, each weighed down with our own fears and thoughts.

We had not yet revealed that my husband and I were certain Adrian was not going to live. While I wondered whether failing to share this knowledge was, perhaps, wrong, instinctively I knew that all of us needed something to hold on to, something to cling to, just for a little while longer—even if that something was false hope. The only point that held any priority was to be with Adrian as soon as we possibly could. How absolutely mad those several hours were! How absolutely mad our world became!

Adrian's horrendous cranial injuries created permanent and haunting visuals. I cannot erase them. He was unrecognizable. Standing over our deeply comatose child, I vowed we would do everything humanly possible to get him out of this mess.

Could he hear us? Did he know we were there? Did he feel us touch him? How deep was his pain? How could this be happening? Was I dreaming? What caused the accident? How can we help him? My God, what is going on here?

We talked to him; we held his hand and stroked his face.

Did it hurt him?

Within hours, it became common knowledge that Adrian was in neurointensive care, in serious condition. The assembly of friends, family, and young people—everyone who knew Adrian wanted to lend their support—was complicated and difficult, but also most comforting. It was necessary to allow those who wanted to, to be at Adrian's side.

Four sleepless and exhausting days later, we made a decision that no parent should ever be faced with. Based on the tests and medical opinions, it felt so right and necessary to discontinue life support. Our unconditional love begged for his suffering to stop.

Nevertheless, a few months after his passing, that decision would cause me deep valleys of self-doubt and guilt. Was our decision morally and ethically sound? My husband and I were at opposite ends of the fence on this. He believed—without doubt—that we helped Adrian die with dignity.

No longer did I know what we did, or for whom. I was tortured.

How we managed to make the funeral arrangements to celebrate Adrian's life, I still cannot fathom. But we did it. Robotically, we kept moving, organizing, breathing, and thinking.

How did we accomplish this? Truly, I believe that, initially, the bereaved do not entirely process the total impact of their tragedies. We are safely buffered until gradually we can acknowledge this new reality. This time is needed to complete the assignment of honouring our loved ones. We want to take care of others. We find ourselves trying to fix everyone and everything.

All this morphs into another chapter, however, as we gradually absorb the truth.

"It is a blessing that you will not know, at the moment of impact, how far-reaching the shock waves will be. Still it is a long time to discover that you are still in shock, still in the infant stages of recovery." —Unknown

Painting Grief:

It would be unfair of me to try to convey what was experienced by my husband, by Adrian's older brother, by other relatives, by Adrian's partner, or by his friends. They alone have that privilege, which I profoundly respect. We each journey the path of grief in our own way and in our own time. We have the right to do so.

What we experience during our personal journeys depends on many things: our individual personalities, how we perceive life and death, our culture, our beliefs, and the relationship we have with the one we have lost. As well, we are impacted by the length of that relationship—how much of a part we played in the life of the deceased, and he/she in ours. The way we have been taught to handle past life events also influences us. How, and by whom, we are supported plays an important role in our ability to process and cope. On top of this, the conditions in which our loved ones die can add layers of complication to our grief.

Without trying to speak for others, I will share a few personal observations. Adrian's brother shut down almost immediately after the funeral. The weight of his emptiness and sorrow was intense. John and I felt every ounce of it. I remember that hugging Anthony felt like wrapping my arms around an inflexible board. He was guarded and distant. I knew he was protecting his dad and me from his own intolerable pain. John became very much task-oriented for several weeks. He was confused and forgetful. Tears were always close, but safely packaged; however, my ears heard where they were released—every morning in the shower— for months.

Adrian's partner was talkative and supportive. Though deeply wounded, she still seemed able to embrace the beauty of life shortly after Adrian's death. The full impact visited her a little later.

While I watched them struggle in their own individual ways, I can tell you, with certainty, I felt shamefully helpless. We were crippled, "travelling" our loss of Adrian profoundly differently. In the infancy of our journeys, our emotional compasses were broken. We were lost. My husband's sisters, and mine, were clearly heartbroken yet supportive. Many relatives and friends seemed comfortable consoling us, while others seemed not to know what to say or do.

Losing our twenty-six-year-old son changed the alignment of my world. Life as I knew it suddenly became foreign and far away. Views and beliefs that once defined me quickly transformed. A future we dreamed of, with Adrian in it, was cancelled. Adrian would not be a dad; he would not be an uncle, a husband, a son, or a brother. My life suddenly separated into before and after: before Adrian died ... after Adrian died.

The pain and grief of this unthinkable loss caused horrific disorientation. There were segments of time during which I really didn't know what I was doing. It felt like my family, and the role each person played, was off balance, fractured, and very disorganized. While I wanted to talk and talk, others needed silence.

I remember standing motionless in the dark, looking through a grey mist of shock, watching the rest of the world move along with the bold audacity of normalcy. Observing friends and relatives continuing regular daily chores and usual activities, I witnessed some people react to trivial occurrences as if they were tragedies. It seemed that I was changing, dissolving—dwelling in a private, lonely, joyless existence. In a room devoid of colour, empty of all emotion except grief, I scrambled to take cover—now I knew that anything could happen. Waiting for another axe to fall, I was scared, I was disabled.

Searching for meaning, I wondered if there was a future to live for. How was I to go on? I was the one who was supposed to keep my child alive—I am the mother. Constricted with guilt and certain that I would not survive without becoming very ill, insane, or both, it seemed to me that this burden of grief was something one really should deal with on one's own. I couldn't. What was wrong with me?

Self-confidence abandoned me. I couldn't remember things. Obsessively, I went over and over the details of the accident, the funeral, our decisions, things that were said, things that weren't said. Exhausted, I worried about Adrian. Was he OK? Where was he—where did he go? Was he alone? Was he cold? Was he hurting? Caught in a panic state, I experienced several confusing, heartbreaking dreams about Adrian. I was certain I was losing my mind ... my self. The rippling effects of Adrian's death were enormous, and the days were long, forlorn, bewildering, and dark.

Within a few short weeks, I knew I could not journey "this" without help. Where would I turn? I had no previous experience, or knowledge, from which I could draw. Yes, I had experienced other losses, but nothing as out of order, and paralyzing, as our son's death—*nothing*! Adrian was supposed to bury his parents ... not the reverse!

As you read about my haunting emotions, questions, and doubts, undeniably they sound dismal and overwhelming. I share this disheartening part of my voyage with purpose.

> *"You must give up the life you planned in order to have the life that is waiting for you." —Joseph Campbell*

Painting Recovery, Healing, Reconciliation:

First, I was rescued by a wonderful, caring neighbour, whom I did not know well, and to whom I remain forever grateful. She was aware of Adrian's death and watched us quietly. One day I reluctantly acknowledged her frantic wave. On a small piece of paper she wrote: "Bereaved Families of Ontario-York Region." At a snail's pace, I began taking infant steps on a long and unavoidable road. Along with becoming involved with this bereavement organization, the help of an exceptional therapist (specializing in the grief of child loss), and the encouragement of friends and family, I made an unconscious decision, opening a door to the arduous task of slowly taking on grief with all its layers.

My outstanding therapist offered a safe harbour, where I wept in a cocoon of warmth without judgment. She accepted all of my ramblings, gently calming me in those early months. With her extraordinary skill and guidance, I came to realize that I was not mad. Although engulfed in torment and hurt, I was normal. Most importantly, I learned that I had the right to grieve and shed rivers of tears for my son. Additionally, I was entitled to search for something more than an existence.

Now that I didn't feel so alone anymore, I began to embrace my sorrow, and to accept that there were no answers to most of my questions.

"It is not how to find the answer, but how to live without one." —*Unknown*

∞

Reading what and when I could—curling up with a book in my own personal refuge—though not for everyone, for me was healing. While I absorbed the experiences of others, I was free to weep, laugh, reject, or accept the written words. No one was watching. No one could correct or shame me. Reading was a safe, cerebral space where I could take my time adjusting to and mapping the alien landscape of grief in complete silence and privacy.

Gaining knowledge about grief normalized it and helped alleviate some of the loneliness associated with the many challenging days, weeks, and months. It validated the intense emotions bombarding me, assuring me that I was not out of my mind, as

I struggled through a world resembling fogged lunacy. Reading helped promote thought; it helped clarify who and where I was.

As well, I returned to hiking, and exercised when energy would permit. Pushing myself, I began to journal, found ways to memorialize and honour Adrian, and spoke his name when others could not, or would not. Concentrating on my son's life, not just his death, I rebuilt a crumbling world the best I could, one small stone at a time.

When I fell, I rested and tried to build again. Travelling a twisted path, with overwhelming ups and downs, I cried and screamed at a God that I was not sure existed. Some days I reinvented family rituals, while I tried to find some bright spots in my world gone grey. As time passed, I began to recognize that, despite everything, and whether I really wanted to or not, I would endure this. And it might be worth a try to explore and find light once again. With this in mind, I kept talking to those who would and could listen.

My husband and I joined a child-loss group with Bereaved Families of Ontario-York Region. We shared our loss with other parents; it helped to learn about their experiences as we blindly stumbled along. It was encouraging to hear or read that there was, perhaps, a future that could make sense. It nurtured us to have someone share not only their collapse but also their slow recovery and healing. Relayed experiences anchored me, just enough, so that I could be still and learn the nature of this path I preferred not to be on. Then, on one particular hike, I came to a deep understanding that without studying and acknowledging this terrain, along with my current surroundings, I would not find my way.

As a nurse, I recognize that the physical and psychological challenges following bereavement are phenomenal. The stress of a loved one's death can endanger health and future productivity. Without assistance from caring, experienced people, risks soar for disease, unemployment, depression, substance abuse, and fractured families.

Many positive results and benefits emerge from people seeking and receiving guidance from dedicated volunteers and professionals. There are excellent programs available, created by those who have been there. Before we can begin to nudge forward, I believe we need validation, acceptance, and a voice. I am extremely fortunate in having had the necessary help to find these avenues—avenues that assist in healing, recovery, and reconstruction. Never will I forget this chapter of discovery. Because of it, I am now a mentor, and a trained facilitator for parents who find themselves mired in a world turned upside down by grief.

∞

"Out of the fragments of the storm you will build new life." —Unknown

Before I go on, I cannot express strongly enough that there is no agenda as to when positive shifts come about. We experience them at different times, and definitely in no particular order. There is some instability to those shifts as well. We lose our loved ones under many different circumstances, making the layers of what we deal with broadly unlike. That said, while each bereaved person suffers in painfully individual ways, still there are countless similarities in our voyages.

Over the years, I have thought a great deal about how my grief continuously matures. The sorrow did not go away, but the force of it softened. Eventually, this unwelcome resident seemed to incorporate itself into my life. I began to respond to it differently, embracing it for what it was, becoming surprisingly familiar with it—now, I feel an odd peace and comfort with grief. My pain decreased, slowly becoming more manageable. And I was relieved to see my husband and son each pace their own shifts and movements toward bright, positive futures.

Grief still visits on the oddest occasions, but I walk and talk with this uninvited companion. The visits are kinder; the walks are shorter and less complicated. A memory has developed of recovering from these waves of sadness. Over time, I have observed that despite the undeniable injustice of Adrian's senseless death, I have actually crept forward with my family. Experiencing joy on occasion, and then more often, I have found delight in being alive. It is a different joy, a different delight.

I was shocked to realize that essentially I was going to come to terms with my grief and find some quality in my life once again. While returning to becoming a useful human being, although in some ways emerging as a different person, I was able to rediscover a measure of cheerfulness. The sadness is always there, in the background, because I can never forget my son, but it no longer dominates my being.

With much courage, determination, and support, my grief had opportunities to mature, and I grew up with it. By allowing myself to befriend grief, sit with it, and explore it, I moved slowly through and reconciled. How could I do otherwise?

Upon reflection, I now know Adrian's death has not cancelled the meaning of his life, nor any personal relationship with him. He remains a son, brother, uncle, nephew, friend, and partner. Wherever he is, wherever we are, our bond with him will forever continue. It can never be severed, as he is carried daily in our memories and in our hearts.

The world is filled with unbelievable tragedy, pain, and loss. There must be a built-in ability inside of us all to cope with—then, eventually, map—the deep valley of heartbreak. If we did not possess this gift, the planet would come to a complete halt; don't you agree?

> *"In the depth of winter, I finally learned that within me*
> *lay an invincible summer." —Albert Camus*

I miss our son, and I miss being his mom, but I am comfortable with where I am—at peace with another shape of grief. One morning, while reflecting on Adrian's early bucket list, I paused at one of his wishes: "Create a method for emotional self-rescue." I pondered; do humans do this instinctively? Have I actually accomplished the creation of a method? I doubt it, but I do know this—there was a time when I flatly rejected the possibility of any happiness, any interests, or a productive future. I was wrong, and for that I am grateful. The great effort of climbing this mountain toward a level of harmony and reconciliation is well worth it. I have new goals, and look forward to them. I am alive, and our son, Adrian, with all of the gifts he left behind, lives as well.

> *Some people awaken us*
> *to new and deeper realizations …*
> *for we gain insight*
> *from the passing whisper of their wisdom.*

> *Some people come into our lives*
> *and leave footprints on our hearts*
> *and we are never ever the same. —Flavia Weedn*

A dragonfly joined me, landing on the bow of my kayak on a warm, tranquil summer day. It flew away, returned, flew away, and returned before it took flight once more to a place I could not see. I wondered again about Adrian.

One of my favourite dragonfly tales is about nymphs living at the bottom of a pond. They were struggling with why friends never returned after climbing the stems of lilies to the top of the water. They were, after all, continually promising each other that the next one called upon to make the journey to the surface would return and reveal what happens, what is really there in the other world.

One nymph made it his mission to report what lay beyond after his ascent. He rested on a lily pad while transforming into a beautiful dragonfly. He then flew with great speed and accuracy back and forth, skimming the water, peering at his friends below—only to discover that even if he could be seen, he would not be recognized as one of them in his new form.

"Not being able to communicate with our loved ones after death is not proof that they do not exist. It does not mean we abandon our relationship with them." —Unknown

Chapter Four

David's Story

Janet Rice

David Alexander Rice:
November 2, 1973–December 19, 2009

"Grief is the price we pay for love."
—HRH Queen Elizabeth II

David's Story

It happened twice last weekend: first at the Metro store and then at a real estate open house. On both occasions, I was pleased to come across a former student who was also a friend. I had not seen either of them in several years. We eagerly exchanged information about academic accomplishments, jobs, husbands, and partners. Of course, the conversation turned to an update about their children, whom I had also taught. And then, inevitably, to my own children, which included some bragging—on my part—about my handsome son Andrew, his lovely wife, and our three wonderful grandsons. In the back of my mind was that ever-present question: "Do I mention David? What about the child I have lost?"

I did not want to elicit sympathy—certainly not after more than three years of grieving, but David was an integral part of our family for thirty-six years. I am not embarrassed, just indecisive. I still cherish him. Should I speak about him? Such is the dilemma of a bereaved mother.

What was the outcome?

In the grocery store, as I explained my dilemma to my friend, it occurred to me that at the time of David's death she was on staff at the funeral home, guiding me through those traumatic events. Here she was, still playing that role—this time, in the grocery aisle. At the open house, the real estate agent took me aside to offer her heartfelt condolences, and we talked about David. I am so thankful for understanding friends.

An "In Memoriam" in a recent *Globe and Mail* says, and I paraphrase, "This is what those who haven't crossed the 'Tropic of Grief'[5] often fail to understand: the fact that someone is dead may mean that they are not alive, but it doesn't mean that they do not exist." To me, this is so true. I am very grateful my community understands that death is not the end.

My deceased son still exists in my heart, and I find comfort in speaking about him. As an optimist, I believe our society is evolving and becoming more sensitive to the subject of death and loss. As a result, we can all gain a better understanding of the "Tropic of Grief."

∞

In order for you to more fully grasp the cause of our grief, I need to share with you a short biography of our son, David. He was tall and handsome, with beautiful dark curly hair and a warm smile. He was a bit reserved, like his family. David was an accomplished pianist and guitarist, sailor, kite-boarder, hockey player, cyclist, and motorcyclist. He was a world traveller and an academic achiever (Ontario Scholar in grade thirteen) who graduated with a degree in civil engineering from the University of Toronto. David was an information-technology computer whiz. He held a great job in a national business institution and had a wonderful future ahead.

Then, in his late twenties, we observed a personality change in David. This led to a heartbreaking diagnosis of schizoaffective

---

5   With grief it may feel (at first) as if you move into different latitudes—a bit like crossing the equator.

disorder. This is, in fact, when grief began to creep into our lives: grief for the lost dreams of a happy, healthy life for our son.

As the disease progressed, David could not work full time, but he did find some meaningful short-term work (for instance, teaching CanBike How to Ride courses for the City). David had great patience and compassion for those children fearful of riding on the busy streets.

During one of those summers, when David was in a good space with his disease, we would meet weekly in the city to do some sightseeing. We had wonderful days together and were very good friends. I have the same warm relationship with Andrew.

But eventually the paranoia and stigma consumed him. Here, I quote our minister's words: "David had the support of a loving family that was cognizant of his mental health issues, and they did everything possible to provide support, including accessing the best medical help. Sadly, it wasn't sufficient because of the depth of his mental illness."

We were constantly in touch with David. Then, one weekend when he came home to visit us, although we did not recognize he was saying goodbye, we did realize, immediately, that he was very ill. Observing his deep distress broke my heart. For hours and hours and hours his brother, father, and I sat with him and begged him to go with us to an emergency ward for treatment. He would have none of it. Ultimately, we acquiesced and let him return to his condo in the city.

He left us to complete suicide (an intentional collision with a train) to escape his demons. It was six days before Christmas, 2009. He was thirty-six years old, and in what should have been the prime of his life. We had tried so hard to intervene and avert this outcome, but to no avail. Now we know that his illness was a textbook case.

Hindsight is 20/20, and as we pieced together the events of the preceding three years, we became aware that we had, in fact, aborted two of David's earlier attempts to take his own life. On those occasions he had agreed to be admitted to hospital, but the effectiveness of the treatment was short-lived; it was a Band-Aid approach.

Those readers with some knowledge of mental illness are aware that forcefully committing/admitting someone to hospital care is a very treacherous business. Often the outcome is a short-term medical benefit with irreparable damage to family relationships. We couldn't take the risk. Of course, we did not know David had been off his medication for probably two months. This time he had meticulously planned every last detail, including the suicide note, and would not be deterred.

Now we live with the consequences of our action/inaction. How do we justify our decisions? What a cross for survivors to bear.

I don't wish to leave the impression that only David's family was present to support him. I want you to know about his remarkable, perceptive, and supportive girlfriend, Norah, who shared the last two years of David's life. Theirs was a romantic relationship, and they were in touch every day. It gave us great comfort to know David had a devoted confidante who was close at hand.

On that fateful weekend, David had not warned Norah of his intentions. We were the ones who had to break the news to her that David was gone. She immediately rushed from her office and caught the next train to our home and family circle. Over the next ten days, which unfortunately included a grim Christmas, Norah was an integral part of all the dreadful meetings with the police, coroner, and funeral home.

Norah's siblings and her best friend travelled from eastern Ontario, Newfoundland, and Nova Scotia to support us. Norah gave a very touching eulogy at the standing-room-only memorial service. I am so grateful she was with us through those terrible days. Not only did Norah comfort us, but I believe it gave her an opportunity to process her own shock and grief as well as become acquainted with the compassionate community in which David had been raised. David's girlfriend continues to be a blessing in our lives. If only there had been a "happily ever after" ending.

∞

Eventually, my wonderful sister and brother-in-law needed to return to their home in British Columbia, and we were faced with cold reality. In those early days and weeks following David's death, my emotional pain was so intense that my chest hurt. With some success, I tried to return to my usual routine, but it felt as if I was sleepwalking. Andrew describes this time as fumbling around a dark room searching for the light switch. We were all groping for help to soothe our pain, but we soon discovered there was no quick fix.

Triggers—reminders of David—bombarded us.

About nine months later, a very perceptive friend observed my state of mind and referred me to an experienced grief counsellor. Over a span of several months, Donna sat with me for an hour each week while I wept and told my story over and over. Somehow the tension was released. I grew stronger and finally could fly on my own again. For her patience and kindness, I will be forever grateful. We continue to keep in touch; we are friends now on a wider spectrum. I was so fortunate to have found Donna. Counsellors can save lives; however, one size does not fit all.

I joined a support group for bereaved mothers, but after four sessions it disintegrated. Fortunately, Andrew and I found a ten-week suicide survivor's course[6] offered at a nearby Distress Centre. Its valuable impact on both of us cannot be overstated. Very skilled leadership of such groups is the key to their success. I hasten to add that a host of loving family members and friends carried me on this journey, and continue to do so to this day.

With the clarity only hindsight can provide, I have come to realize that every member of our family circle has been profoundly changed by David's death. Bereavement is a strange and ever-changing experience, further complicated by the fact that each person responds and reacts at a different rate and in a different way. Our family was, and continues to be, a devoted and loving circle. But now we tread more carefully; we perceive behaviour in each other prompted by the uglies of grief: sorrow, anger, guilt, and penetrating pain. Now my great fear is that I might, unintentionally, alienate someone in our family unit or misinterpret a remark or a response.

The cruel loss of one member has jarred me with the realization of the immeasurable value and significance of our remaining family members. We are the only people on earth who feel the true impact of this tragedy. We need each other, even if only in silence. We also need space, tolerance, love; those we have—thank God.

How are we coping with the uglies of grief?

Every day a trigger will remind one or all of us of our great loss, and our sorrow returns like a dark shadow. Even now, my husband suffers from ongoing guilt, though he could not have been a more devoted and conscientious father.

Andrew sought counselling for anger in order to restore a healthier emotional balance, particularly with his wife and children. I am so proud to say he has made tremendous progress in

---

6 Volunteer-based support groups for surviving victims of completed suicide are available in many jurisdictions and in various countries. Please reach out for the help you need.

recovering his equilibrium. He is an exceptional husband and a devoted father to our grandsons, who adore him.

Personally, I also suffer from guilt, but it is tempered by the fact that I do not know what else we could have done as a family to support David. Of course, our provincial privacy laws impacted that dilemma. My son was an adult in his thirties and he lived an hour from our home. We, as his parents, had no legal right to his medical records. Mental illness is so awful; family and friends feel impotent in so many ways. My greatest struggle, however, has been with anger—in only one regard: the sorry state of health care for the mentally ill. As David's condition worsened, as a family we journeyed into a world that was completely foreign to us. To our utter dismay, we discovered a dreadful scarcity of available professionals: psychiatrists, psychologists, social workers, and community support services.

Fortunately, we were in a position in which we could provide safe housing, privacy, and all the necessities of life that our son deserved. We were less successful in manoeuvring within the health care system. Here I must acknowledge some of the complicating issues, as follows:

- Anosognosia—a deficit of awareness in the patient that he actually is ill, including frontal lobe dysfunction and denial.
- Privacy laws—which prevent parents of adult children from accessing/sharing medical information. This one really baffles me. Who does the province think is doing the caregiving? The health care services did a fine job of protecting David's privacy—he did not receive the treatment he needed, and he died.
- Lack of integrated support—in an ideal world, a team of medical professionals of all stripes and supporting counsellors would form a team with the patient and his/her

family—each with their own role to play. This model is used
successfully in palliative care, but we have yet to carry over
this concept to the mentally ill. Subsequently, they linger
in emergency rooms with overlapping physical and mental
symptoms, and are often ignored. Why? Because we don't
know enough about the functioning of the human brain
or the treatment that will be most effective. (Please refer
to the comments that follow regarding the work at The
Royal Ottawa.)

- Stigma—it is now apparent that cancer has touched almost
every family. If the veil of secrecy was lifted, I believe we
would find that the incidence of mental illness is close
behind. An estimated 6.7 million Canadians (one in five)
suffer from mental health problems at any given time. There
are so many of us with personal tragedies; those involving
mental illness have been kept in the closet far too long.

- Bricks and mortar—I believe that more of the monies
spent on fancy hospital foyers and other aesthetics could be
redirected to outpatient follow-up services in the community for the mentally ill. Patients with mental illnesses are
routinely released from hospital with completely inadequate
support systems. It is criminal! The result is what I call the
revolving door syndrome. Our David was intelligent and
perceptive, and he recognized this sequence of events.

∞

Thankfully, I glimpse signs of positive change, which I watch
with keen interest. I take comfort in the hope that the following
resources, and many others, will lead to an easier journey—easier

for those yet to travel this tragic path of loss involving mental illness, and possible suicide...

- The work of Senator Michael Kirby on the Mental Health Commission—several projects are evolving from this report, including *Out of the Shadows at Last*, *At Home/Chez Soi*, and *Partners for Mental Health*. Each program has a specific thrust; the last is dedicated to the prevention of youth suicide.
- The ambitious, successful outreach and in-house programs offered by The Royal Ottawa Mental Health Institute: Statistics prove that early onset of illness often presents in the teenage years. The Royal works with high school youth, focusing on de-stigmatizing mental problems through educational programs. The mandate at The Royal is simply to get more people living with mental illness into recovery faster. Their work includes advocacy, education, treatment, and research—a broad spectrum.
- The annual Bell Canada "Let's Talk" initiative, featuring spokesperson and Olympian Clara Hughes, is a wonderful example of corporations stepping up to raise funds and awareness—again offering education and de-stigmatization. It is heartwarming for me to observe the response from the public.
- In his newspaper column, "Second Opinion," in the *Globe and Mail*, Andre Picard writes knowledgeably about health care, and frequently about the treatment of the mentally ill.
- Our local Distress Centre and Community Care COPE (CCD) program offers desperately needed support services to those in distress, survivors, and their families.

∞

Death is always touched by the conditions surrounding it. Today, as I write, I am acutely aware that next month brings us to the fourth anniversary of David's death. As we work our way through the month, again we will relive the grim circumstances of our son's illness and death. Anniversaries are tough. I have to keep reminding myself that David has been freed from his valiant struggles and is at peace.

As I look ahead, it is now my task to search for my own peaceful place: a place in which I can move forward with my life, holding David's memory in my heart. This is my new normal. I paraphrase television personality Dr. Phil McGraw: "Time does not heal all wounds. It is what you do with that time that will determine the extent of your healing."

I must maintain my composure to do what I really want to do: use my gifts to pay it forward to others in needy circumstances, as a way of acknowledging the many, many acts of kindness shown to me in my own bereavement. The sharp physical pain in our hearts has been replaced by a soft ache. Grief is the price we pay for love, and love never ends.

A Poem Break

Desiderata

Go placidly amid the noise and the haste,
and remember what peace there may be in silence.
As far as possible, without surrender,
be on good terms with all persons.

Speak your truth quietly and clearly;
and listen to others,
even to the dull and the ignorant;
they too have their story.

Avoid loud and aggressive persons;
they are vexatious to the spirit.
If you compare yourself with others,
you may become vain or bitter,
for always there will be greater and lesser persons than yourself.

Enjoy your achievements as well as your plans.
Keep interested in your own career, however humble;
it is a real possession in the changing fortunes of time.

Desiderata (continued)

Exercise caution in your business affairs,
for the world is full of trickery.
But let this not blind you to what virtue there is;
many persons strive for high ideals,
and everywhere life is full of heroism.

Be yourself. Especially do not feign affection.
Neither be cynical about love,
for in the face of all aridity and disenchantment,
it is as perennial as the grass.

Take kindly the counsel of the years,
gracefully surrendering the things of youth.

Nurture strength of spirit to shield you in sudden misfortune.
But do not distress yourself with dark imaginings.
Many fears are born of fatigue and loneliness.

Beyond a wholesome discipline,
be gentle with yourself.
You are a child of the universe
no less than the trees and the stars;
you have a right to be here.

A Poem Break

And whether or not it is clear to you,
no doubt the universe is unfolding as it should.
Therefore be at peace with God,
whatever you conceive Him to be.
And whatever your labors and aspirations,
in the noisy confusion of life,
keep peace in your soul.
With all its sham, drudgery, and broken dreams,
it is still a beautiful world.
Be cheerful. Strive to be happy.

By Max Ehrmann, written in 1927

Window Washer Sings at the Terminal

His song makes me think
of green hills with little green stalks
upright, wind leaning. Look.
He is a sparrow in those fields,
trilling the echo of his lyrics,
flapping from blade to blade across
the panes of glass, the walls,
until he lands, easing. His song has edged us
to the clarity of his sweet loss and the window
is ready now for wings to fly through it.

By Catherine Graham

The Ritual

Surrounded by green's dark, the day's wind
gathered in a knot, we walk the country road after dinner
the flush of wine scoring our skin.
The tingle, after fireworks that we can't see,
hums through the palms of our hands.
We don't have to talk if you don't want to,
but we do in whispers when the woods blink back.
Brief, pale, yellow, we've arrived at the ritual. Come now.
Right here.

By Catherine Graham

Six Healing Prayers:

Reflections clear on waters still; the images' shimmering hue and form.
When breezes blow to blur from sight the trees they stand,
wait out the storm …

∞

And when all warring sense has calmed to once again be still
and know;
The mighty pine, it stands unharmed by mortal thought's sugges-
tive blow.

A Poem Break

∞

Perfect child of Love and grace, wipe the teardrops from your face.
The sun shines bright through window yon.
Today's the gift of thoughtful dawn.

∞

All systems freely flow, for you are rightly made. A cherished child of
Love. No need to feel afraid ...

∞

No beginning and no end, your life's in Spirit's care.
Eternal Mind defines what's true and Truth is real right here.

∞

Silent reverence, gift of sight, present help in day or night.
Eternal Life that knows no miles walks hand in hand with you,
Her child.

By Kelly Foxton

Chapter Five

Russell's Story

Beverley Ogus

Russell Alan Ogus:
February 17, 1970–May 8, 1989

"A time to break down, a time to build up;
a time to weep and a time to laugh;
a time to mourn..."
—Ecclesiastes 3:4

Russell's Story

Inexplicably, the minute I arrived home, I could hear a car running in the closed garage.

Dear God, it must be Russell; no one else is home.

In complete confusion and panic, I pounded on the locked door, immediately screaming, "Russell, what are you doing? Are you crazy?"

"Stop!"

"Open this door right now!"

∞

Monday, May 8, 1989, was a rainy, cloudy, totally miserable day. At this place in time, I was a forty-four-year-old mother of four sons, a former psychiatric nurse experiencing success in running my own company, recently honoured for business achievements.

But this particular afternoon, normal successes were achingly remote. Russell was top of my mind. Leaving my office early, I was rushing home to take this nineteen-year-old to the family doctor. He had been sick for a week with a terrible cough. When he had visited the doctor on his own the week before, the diagnosis was viral—no treatment. I needed to confirm it for myself since he had been sounding much worse.

Russell was completing grade thirteen. Despite his aptitude, his marks were not great; chances were he would not be accepted to a university of his choice. On that long silent drive from Newmarket to our home in Toronto, I fretted. It felt as if Russell was floundering.

Last Saturday afternoon, when my husband David and I arrived home from a bar mitzvah, we found that despite begging Russell not to teach his swimming class, he had done it his way and gone. An argument ensued, to do with Russell wanting to quit school, leave home, and find a job. There was no way that I could agree to this. Then, on Saturday night, in spite of his illness, he went out and got drunk. Russell had not done this before. The bouncer phoned our house, wanting to send Russell home in a taxi. David agreed to cover the cab fare, and Russell was dropped off, vomiting and very ill. His dad cleaned up, threw the dirty laundry into the wash, and tucked Russell into bed. I slept through the entire episode. The next day we talked about all of this with Russell, reminiscing about our own inept experiments with alcohol as teenagers. What was happening to our cherished little boy?

∞

Russell, the third of our four sons, was born when his oldest brother, Brian, was three-and-a-half years old and his older brother Aaron two-and-a-half. Russell seemed more dependent on me than his brothers had been. Perhaps, since Brian and Aaron were so close in age, they were more involved with each other.

For almost six years, Russell basked as the youngest and we spent a great deal of individual time together. When I suffered an ectopic pregnancy shortly after his second birthday it appeared that he would be the final addition to our family. Fate allowed a fourth brother; just before Russell's sixth birthday, Matthew was born. No longer was he the baby; Russell needed to share Mom with his infant brother too.

∞

Driving home on that rainy Monday, reliving these vivid memories, I could not stop agonizing that my son needed help. That very afternoon I resolved to accelerate his support. Tragically, he made his decision first.

Upon finding Russell, pain exploded in every cell of my body. Shock, horror, disbelief, and blinding fear instantaneously extinguished any fleeting flashes of pride in former accomplishments.

After I smashed the garage window and called 9-1-1, wild, panicky voices collided inside of my head.

"My life is over."

"How could Russell do this to himself?"

"How could Russell do this to us?"

My first contact with another person was with a young policeman, to whom I blurted, "I was a psychiatric nurse—I should have known ..."

Fused with the pervasive sorrow of Russell's death, my sense of responsibility was profound. Who would be blamed for this tragedy if not the mother? Why would Russell not have come to his father or to me? Why did I not recognize his suicidal symptoms? My thoughts overran each other ...

People will think that I gave up my sons for my career.

Maybe if I had stayed home longer than the eleven years I was a full-time mother, Russell would have reached out when he needed me most. Perhaps I could have saved Russell, but I was not there. These were my punishing self-examinations during the first days, weeks, and months—bleeding into the upcoming years.

Our son's shocking death was beyond devastating. With no solace to be found, the aftermath overwhelmed us. Who could we discuss our feelings with? No one—the topic of suicide was untouchable. Envisioning that I had to contain it all inside of me, I was surrounded by an uneasy silence. I remained fearful of the judgement of others—judgement I imagined was waiting to name me. Paralleling my feelings of guilt was anger. Or was it furor and despair?

Could Russell not have waited one more day, when the warm sunshine might have stolen his darkness? Perhaps one more day would have changed his mind? Why did he react so irreversibly? Urgently, I sought to rewrite this bleak outcome, as brilliant white light shone on Russell's funeral, and on our endless tears.

Additionally, I was driven by a compulsion to monitor my family obsessively—lest another, in our diminishing number, have similar ideas. In truth, I was overcome and longed to vanish—to sink into the ground alongside my son. Surely he must have known how much we loved him. The intensity of my loss and regret was intermingled with self-blame and shame. Russell was angry with me because I had refused to let him quit school, move out, and get a job. But did our son fully understand that his actions would be final?

∞

My fevered brain returned ruthlessly to May 8. In desolation, over and again, I relived that brutal day. As I had pounded on the garage door, screaming and raging at Russell, panic and terror had threatened to paralyze me. And then, at once, the former nurse resurfaced. With the dissociation of numbing shock, on auto-pilot I had called 9-1-1. Unearthing strength far beyond my own, I had smashed the garage window. Knowing nothing of where David stored his tools, I had found the hammer and broken into Russell's car.

He was warm! Could Russell be alive? Please, please be alive! Very soon I learned that it was all too late. In my anguish, I did not shut off his car. The policeman, who arrived shortly, switched off the ignition. Anger roared through my body; once spent, it evaded me for months, as I lived frozen in shock and hopelessness.

We live in a society that often stigmatizes mental illness and, certainly, the taking of your own life. What were people thinking … did they believe suicide was hereditary?

To what would our other children be subjected, and how would their peers react to the completed suicide of their brother? Would our sons find a place, in the midst of friends, to share their grief? Or would opinions of disgrace prevent them from finding meaningful relationships? What about David and me? What were our friends and associates thinking? What was our extended family thinking? No one said anything. My questions were endless; the silence was deafening.

In retrospect, I am not surprised at how frantic I was. I feared being alone and was afraid to be with others. I hated my world more each morning when I awoke. Every night I parked my car in the place where Russell had died, imagining that the door would slam shut and I would be stuck in that same spot.

While desperate for the pain to end, I was gripped by fear for my family. A frenzied worry persisted that someone else might be planning a suicide. My assumed burden obliged me to stay ever vigilant; Russell had shown how easily it could be done.

Driving my children and David nuts, I had to know where they were and what they were doing every moment of every day. If anyone was missing for a few minutes, I was convinced they were dead. Cell phones were not common then, so I depended on my family to let me know if they would be late. When someone was delayed and did not call, I endured many moments of abject terror, convinced the worst had happened. Eventually I would learn that these panicky, unfounded fears—so alarming to experience—occur quite often, as a natural part of grief following a traumatic, unexpected death.

∞

Along with the deep despondency of sorrow, I was shamed by Russell's fatal act. Always I had trusted that I was a good mother. Loving my children, I had happily cared for them and willingly devoted the better part of my adult life to them. Where did I fail? Tormented by wild imaginings, with an apprehension that every-one saw me as the murderer of my son, I wondered how I would continue to live with myself, or attempt to face the outside world.

During the darkest hours, I thought, "If only fate could put me out of my misery." Mercifully, I had neither the energy nor the misguided courage to pursue these bleak, destructive fanta-sies. Fortunately, possessing an intense concern for my family, I was constrained from inflicting more of the same pain on those I dearly loved.

Later, in therapy, I would discover that thoughts of self-harm, as disturbing as they can be, are not unusual for bereaved parents. Learning to live with the death of a child can be a lifetime journey. It becomes essential to reach out for the help you need.

∞

Russell left to survive him a family who loved him: three brothers (Brian, twenty-three; Aaron, twenty-two; Matthew, thirteen); his father and me; four grandparents; aunts, uncles, and cousins. What happened to us?

Brian sobbed his heart out during the shiva.[7] And then he rallied, as best he could, to comfort his parents. Three months later he left home to live with his girlfriend, as previously planned. With a yearning for life to continue as normally as possible, I was petrified to stand in anyone's way.

Aaron was silent. He had been close to Russell too, and traumatic emotions besieged him. Nonetheless, somehow he needed to return to his university to piece together the continuing semester, and this he did. Despite the painful burdens of shock and grief, Aaron successfully completed his year.

Now Matthew was the only child at home with two grieving parents. He, unlike his brothers, could be coerced to get some help. Three months later, he participated in a siblings' group, where his fears, as well as his feelings of anger and sorrow, could be validated. In addition, we conceded that he could get a pet. Ricky the Labrador retriever provided much comfort to us all. Previously, I had informed my family that either they could have a pet or a mother. In truth, I had been really nervous around dogs; at this time, I was more apprehensive of refusing.

David cried endlessly, for days. Neither our children nor I had ever seen him cry. In abject despair, he resigned from his twenty-five-year career as a chartered accountant, senior partner, in a successful practice.

Although broken on the inside, my façade portrayed me as pulled together—in control. While struggling to hold the fragments of my life in place, I was convinced that it was up to me to

---

7 Shiva: in Judaism, a formal period of seven days of mourning for a deceased relative.

stay strong, be the backbone of this injured family. It felt vital that my grief remain restrained, under tight rigid wraps. If I peeked too closely, our world would collapse. We would fall apart. Barely could I touch the tip of my raging emotions; clinging to denial, I buried my heartbreak in trying to run my business. Facing the reality of Russell's death loomed as insurmountable. In my heart of hearts, I knew I urgently needed help.

Thankfully, I turned to Bereaved Families of Ontario and joined a mothers' group. What a phenomenal relief to have my feelings validated. No one else in my group had lost a child to suicide, but all had experienced feelings of guilt, anger, and isolation. Our society cannot deal with the death of a child much better than it deals with suicide.

As well, we reached out to Survivors' Support—an organization for survivors of suicide. Volunteers came to our home to talk to anyone in the family who wanted to share. The boys ran, except for one night, which they deemed enough for them. But these brave people were very comforting to David and me.

David joined a fathers' group at Bereaved Families. He found these sessions helpful and supportive. Then we began seeing a psychiatrist to try to cope with our grief together, but that didn't work for me. David stayed with the doctor and I moved on, fearing that with my pain this resolutely buried, I would not make it without constant, determined support. Luckily, I found an excellent psychoanalyst[8] who could stand with me in my sorrow. Without this gifted professional, I sense that I may not have survived. Or, at the very least, I could not have been supportive to my family in any helpful fashion. My therapist's office was a safe place where I began to deal with my grief as well as my suicidal thoughts.

---

8 Psychoanalysts and/or grief therapists are personal choices. However, the "right one" can be life-affirming while coping with traumatic loss. Keep an open mind and continue to reach out for what you need.

∞

As part of working through my trauma, I wrote to Russell—letters that may give you a clearer picture of our family's journey. Perhaps I can share two of them now. The first letter was written in 1991, two years after Russell's suicide. By this time, I was working diligently to share my true feelings.

During my continuing grief work, I grasped that two years are "early days" in a bereaved parent's journey. Ultimately, I recognized—as perhaps you have too—that there are many ups and downs with grief. The path to healing may be indirect and jarring, while you wade through the waves of guilt and despair accompanying a grievous loss.

First letter to Russell (written in April 1991)

Dear Russell,

Where are you? Two years since you took your own life, and still it is wrenching for me to write. I am working to forgive myself for not saving you, also to let go of my anger—anger at me and at you. Shortly after the catastrophic day of your death, your four-year-old cousin burst into your Aunt Marcee's bedroom with a huge bag of toys, demanding, "Mommy, I know that Russell is dead, but I have all of these broken toys; when is he coming back to fix them?"

I need to ask the same thing: "When are you coming back?" In my head I understand, but with my heart I watch for you.

Early in our marriage, your dad and I were told by our doctors that it was unlikely we could ever have children. We were devastated! Yet, miraculously, we had four sons—each of you a miracle, one of a kind.

As a toddler, you were so outgoing that you engaged everyone from the moment you mastered speech. As you grew, you continued to be friendly, caring, and eager for peace to reign—ready to intercede at the first sign of conflict. You wanted your family, friends, and colleagues on the same page, loving each other and getting along. With infectious humour, you would get us laughing along with you and at your silly antics.

Sometimes, teasingly, I would ask, "So who is going to look after me, once I'm old and unable to care for myself?" You would jump in, "I will, I will!" Your brothers willingly supported this concept. "Don't worry, Mom, Russell will look after you."

An empathetic champion for the less fortunate, you were proactive in helping wherever you could. Realizing too late how vulnerable you were, I was helpless to bolster that fragile person hidden under your veneer of confidence and rebellion. Emotionally, you were a boy who needed a loving mother; conversely, you were an adult who rejected me. Hugging you, listening to you, I was so afraid of treating you like a baby. You were making noises of a lust for independence, but the cries were those of a child.

Now I feel that I understand a little more, but two short years ago I was at a loss. Russell, you were more troubled than we suspected. It is heartrending to recall how useless my attempts were to convince you to talk to a professional. I could have helped you. What possible harm would there have been?

You were so adamant that you were fine that reluctantly I trusted—assuring myself I was overreacting because, as a mom, I needed to soften your path through life. In our family, between your dad and you four boys, almost daily I was reproved by one or another, "You're over-dramatizing, fussing us way too much."

Russell, I am sorry, with my whole heart, that I wasn't intuitive enough to see beneath the surface of you. Any time your father and I admonished you, we glimpsed your hurt. But you stopped us in our tracks. We were confused by your ambiguous behavior, and could not grasp what you were looking for. In retrospect, perhaps you were seeking protection—if this was so, we are shattered that you did not ask.

Having lived through your older brothers' struggles, with their volatile teenage angst, we had faith that you too would survive these challenging years and ultimately flourish. Of course you would; how could you not? Yet here we are, and there you are—your tragic death haunts us still. It was far too soon for you to leave us. We pray that you have found peace.

In honour of you, I search for blessings in the midst of your loss. And even though, on my blackest days, it feels as if my life is over, day by day I promise you that I will reach out and find a way to endure this pain. We miss you. Love, Mom

∞

Second letter (February 17, 1994)

Happy twenty-fourth birthday, Russell—this is a day when I feel most alone. Your birthday is too painful for your father and brothers to mark. We each grieve differently, but I wish we could share our feelings a little more. Today I let go of your loss long enough to cherish the moments we shared.

My time was divided, but you knew how to get that extra hug, one more cuddle. Nonetheless, you changed—our family changed. What was missing? Perhaps we were stuck in the crazy busyness of life. I do not know. But at this very moment, it does not matter—I have chosen to spend the day with you.

By now, you should have an undergraduate degree. You had the potential. As I watch your friends and contemporaries growing older, moving ahead with their lives, I yearn for what might have been for you. Your friend Mitchell is in his third year of medical school. We reconnected at Matthew's high school graduation. Mitchell looks great and has a pretty girlfriend. We hugged and parted with tears.

Whenever I go to the cemetery there are flowers on your grave. Who, besides me, comes to see you almost five years later? With your considerate ways, and eager smiles, so many loved you. If only you had loved yourself as much.

Let me tell you more about your brothers.

Matthew is eighteen and unsure what to do with his life. He's working at Consolidated Bottle until camp. It seems this family business plays a pivotal role. Sometimes I wonder what might have been if I had found the courage to let you to leave school and work there as you wanted. With distance and perspective, I suspect you would have tired and moved on. Back then I did not trust, fearing that you would forfeit your education with the completion of high school only scant months away. Tragically, this all is irrelevant now.

Aaron, already twenty-seven, is off to the west chasing his dreams in the high-tech universe. You are important to him and, when he visits home, I feel the pain of his loss. Brian and Christine married in 1991; she has been compassionate in helping us cope with your suicide, and will be our only daughter-in-law who knew you. They seem a happy couple—a new house, two new cars, and a cat too. Now, I suppose, I am a cat Bubie.[9] Still, as settled as they are, they mourn your "Russell-spot" in their lives.

---

9 Bubie: Jewish grandmother

Your dad—well, your death almost did him in! He left his practice shortly after you died; he totally fell apart and then joined my business at Nutrisystem. We argued and bickered, the accountant and the entrepreneur. When the economy turned and Nutrisystem was over for me, your dad went to work for a former client in the client's grocery business. As of 1994, he's still there.

Finally, here's the incongruity—I am back at Consolidated Bottle, selling bottles and caps, busy doing what I forbade you to do. Life is stranger and much sadder than fiction. What remains feels crucial for me to share: the trauma of losing you, coupled with my self-inflicted pressure to take care of everyone else, almost led to my own demise.

Though grief work has furthered my insight, I am left with unanswered questions about why you died at your own hand— perhaps I will always have these. Now my big choice is to go on to live the rest of my life as best I can. Slowly, I am learning how to take care of myself too.

We miss your pranks, your peacekeeping, your love, and even your anger. Despite your physical absence, you are a part of us and we are grateful for the time we had together. Love, Mom

∞

Following are paraphrased excerpts from my 1995 speech, "Aftermath of a Tragic Death: Unique Aspects of a Survivor's Grief," presented to the Bereavement Ontario Network. My talk took place a year after Russell's second letter, six years after his suicide. While I share how we are managing as a family, you will encounter repetition; however, I hope that you experience validation too …

Brian and Christine moved west early in 1995. I hoped they might reach out for help, but they have each other and perhaps that is enough. Aaron pursued his career even more intensely. As a mom, I worry that he runs from his pain, but then again, I know all about running. Matthew is away at university. I sense that he longs for the carefree, fun-loving parents he enjoyed for the first thirteen years of his life. Still, he is the only one of our sons who can talk openly about his brother's suicide and its impact on his life.

My business died with the economy. I sold out in 1993, spending the next year and a half unemployed and depressed. Grief is patient. With no outlet for escape, there was little choice for me but to work with my true feelings. I had nowhere to run, nowhere to hide.

Now, in 1995, I am more content to be working again, selling on the road. Most of my customers know nothing of Russell's death; consequently, I don't have to deal with my grief during working hours. Nor do I need to fret about what someone might be thinking of me.

Facilitating groups at Bereaved Families of Ontario has been helpful for me. This volunteer work has evolved into an important part of my healing. I am trying, as best I can, to inch forward with my life—bit by bit putting our traumatic tragedy behind me. Most importantly, I no longer take full responsibility for Russell's suicide. I accept that he was not well.

Having stood at the edge of that same cliff many times over the past six years, I realize how ill one has to be to jump. Although I understand, too well, the impact and devastation of that fatal decision on others, I doubt very much that our son did. No longer am I angry at him. In his confusion, sorrowfully, he may have felt that he was doing us a favour. I strive to focus on the joyful times we shared in Russell's life, individually with him and together as a family. While I am no longer ashamed of how my son died, even today I cope with the discomfort of others—when, amongst relatives and friends, there is mention of Russell's name and the circumstances of his death.

One of my missions is to try to educate people in my world that suicide is the end of a chronic illness, which tragically has become lethal, and not the selfish act so many consider it to be.

At times I feel isolated. Our three oldest sons are far away; two are separated from us geographically, Russell, regretfully by death. Matthew, unsurprisingly, is wound up in his own world. My husband, David, is preoccupied with the struggles of finding his way. He regrets packing in his career—so far nothing has fit him that well.

Even with our love for one another, often we are as singular as islands—each coping differently, alone. Grief can be like that. However, I have been blessed with the unconditional support and empathy of two dedicated professionals, saving me from myself, guiding me through these most difficult six years.

Having said all of the above, and reflecting upon the shared experiences of the groups I have facilitated, I wonder if the aftermath of Russell's suicide is much different from others' experiences in respect to the deaths of their children. Guilt, despair, anger, regret, and isolation seem common themes, whether the loss is due to illness, accident, murder, or suicide.

Just the same, it surprises me how quickly group participants have rallied to tell me that what I have suffered is the worst loss. One of my group members declared, "Suicide is self-murder. What could be worse?"

Despite my growth, the negative aftermath of Russell's completed suicide lingers. I catch myself analyzing life's challenges. I find myself questioning whether they were precipitated by his death, from the shifts in our lifestyles and relationships to the various deviations from our individual career paths, some of which have turned our world upside down.

As of 1995 (over all the wrenches of these six tough years), the composing of this presentation stands as one of my challenges. Doing so demanded digging up feelings that I prayed had been put to bed. While these reflections have been therapeutic, they have been raw and sorrowful too. Perhaps, with the death of a child, the healing is rarely complete, but rather a continuing journey of learning and reconciliation.

Russell broke the rules of order by ending his own life.

When remnants of guilt, anger, and shame hover over me, as sometimes they do, I seek solace in my sincere belief that at the time I was the best mother I knew how to be.

My son's parting gift to us was the impetus to grow from our trauma. While I endeavour to define my growth, today I stand here before you as both a teacher and a student. Thank you for your attention and kind support.

∞

*Every blade of grass has an angel that bends over it
and whispers "Grow, Grow." —The Talmud*

As the years move by, the suicide of a child can be reminiscent of a flood roaring through the lifecycle of the family, tossing survivors indiscriminately, compromising much.

Some acquaintances have assured us, "Thank heaven you have other sons," not comprehending the stabbing insensitivity of their words. Of course, it is a blessing to have other children; however, each child is an individual. One cannot take the place of another, nor would we want them to.

Though we are not the same people we were before, through it all our family has forged a way forward—toward life, toward happiness. There are no timelines for our grief journey; it is an individual path. For myself, once I reached outward for the help I needed, I began to explore a healing course. With the insights of grief work, I have learned that fathers, mothers, and siblings grieve differently; also that we cannot fix one another no matter how much we might like to. It is love, coupled with acceptance of our differences that helps us.

During my volunteer work—together with further education—I have faced in person, and studied in articles, scenarios where bereaved brothers and sisters have vented their worries that, for their parents, it seemed to be all about the dead child rather then about "them" (the ones who remain). They agonize, "What about me?" When this is the case, terrible guilt may be suffered, for momentary lapses into jealousy, toward a sibling who has died. While conflicting emotions can be distressing to experience, they are a normal part of grief and it helps to share with those who understand.

∞

Third letter to Russell (December 15, 2013)

Dear Russell,

Never are you far from my thoughts, even though it has been years since I have written to you.

So much has changed ... where do I start? ... Today, as an active psychotherapist, in my fourteenth year of practice, I'm providing grief counselling, individual therapy, and helping survivors of suicide go on with their lives. The shock of your death forcibly pushed me to find meaning in my own life. Eventually, I went back to school, in an attempt to make something useful from the sorrow of your loss.

Facilitating self-help groups at Bereaved Families gave me purpose, along with a safe place to talk about you. Concurrently, I continued in therapy, searching for myself and taking baby steps toward coping with your suicide. It was there (in therapy) that I decided I wanted to help others who were struggling with their losses. So I studied purposefully, determined to learn more.

When I started my own practice, the clients came. I don't know ... they just came. I became instantly engaged—for the first time in such long time—and I have been enjoying my work, finding meaning, and feeling fulfilled. No doubt I have you to thank for my career change, although I'd give it back in a heartbeat to have you here.

Russell, as you likely know, your three brothers are now fathers themselves. I am not just a cat Bubie anymore: eight lovely grandchildren, four dogs, two cats, a horse, and a pony. In this, we are blessed. Despite the distances, we try to gather at the cottage for at least one family week. This summer will be special, as we will be celebrating our fiftieth wedding anniversary, along with my seventieth birthday.

Your dad has been working hard as a financial planner/ stockbroker for the past eighteen years. He loves his work. There are no plans for either of us to retire just yet.

Zaida[10] Maxie died in 2001. You were the apple of his eye; he saw much of himself in you. Bubie Rosie is still alive at ninety-five years of age. Do you recall your indulged relationship with her—how, inevitably, you could get your Bubie to spring for that extra special something?

Nanny and Pappa also have died. Russell, you left behind four devastated grandparents who struggled to reconcile themselves to your untimely death while they still lived.

Consolidated Bottle no longer is in our family—a very long story for another day...

Your eight nieces and nephews are asking about you, and the cause of your death. I have said (as I believe) that you were very ill and will tell them, when they ask more questions, that your illness was depression that became terminal.

Eventually, we bought a house with a pool—your dream come true, you so loved to swim.

Oh, I do wonder where you would be, and what you would be doing. You would be forty-three years old by now; would you be married? Would you have children? It has been almost twenty-five years, yet you are with us during our joyous events as well as in our sad moments.

Touchingly, your cousins have not forgotten how you helped fix their toys. You were their hero. Two of your nephews bear your name, and in our gatherings there are the "Russell Stories," which form a part of the family dialogue—an integral piece of the family glue. Our lives have been impacted by you; you have

---

10   Zaida: Jewish grandfather

made a mark on generations past, present, and future. Thank you for our time together. Love, Mom

∞

Today, as I reflect over these many years, I am grateful that, individually and as a family, we have found healing ways to live with the pain of losing Russell, to fulfill our lives—to find happiness. This continuing journey has clarified many ideas for me. Before I close, I would like to share a few of my perceptions with you.

Russell taught us to hold our special people closer, to let them know how dear they are; although we have this moment, we cannot count on more—so make each one matter. After shelter and food, it has been proven to me that meaning is an essential part of life.

In addition, no matter how raw to express and to feel, in grief there are no wrong emotions, as long as you do not hurt yourself, or anyone else. Understandably, all humans seek to avoid sorrow; nonetheless, grief is patient and will wait relentlessly for you to stop running.

Ultimately, it is healing and in fact essential to embrace your true feelings—to speak about your pain. Continue to reach out for the help you need, being as kind as you can—most importantly, to yourself.

Be realistic in your expectations. The death of a child is a death out of the order of life. As you work diligently to find your way, purpose and joy are waiting if you don't give up. Please choose life and love; I have.

Chapter Six

Sean's Story

Kathleen Stevens

Sean Angus Duncan:
May 8, 1977–June 8, 2012

"Until we meet again, may God hold you in the hollow of His hand."
—Excerpt from an Irish blessing, engraved on the plaque of
Sean's columbarium.

Sean's Story

I woke on the morning of June 8, 2012 never suspecting that my life would be profoundly and forever altered that evening. Our lack of awareness, as human beings, of what the future holds allows us to go about our lives feeling somewhat protected from what could be and eventually will be. By this, I mean that although we know that we and our loved ones eventually will die, many of us live a life of denial.

The death of someone else's loved one—or worse, of their child—is not related to our own life but to other people's lives. When we hear about the death of a child, most of us breathe a sigh of relief and thank God that it wasn't one of ours. Unfortunately, living in this state of denial makes us less likely to live in the moment, enjoying it fully and knowing that it is a gift. We live as if we have life forever, have our children forever. This is just not true, as I have discovered. No matter what the circumstances (or the choices he made), it never occurred to me that my son, Sean, would die on this day, at the age of thirty-five. I just did not expect it. It blindsided me completely.

Truly, I had a fantastic day on June 8, 2012. Often I'm torn and conflicted when I think of that day: my happiness throughout the daylight hours and my utter devastation that night. Working from home, I accomplished quite a lot on a project for work. It was one of those times when everything just seemed to fall into place. I finished my workday feeling productive, self-sufficient, and doubly happy that it was Friday. Also, I was looking forward to spending the weekend with my husband, Robert.

My daughter, Kelly, called around 4:00 p.m. to tell me that her father had offered her a couch he no longer needed. I suggested I drive her to pick it up. Liam, my four-year-old grandson, would come with us. As well, I was happy that day because I get along very well with Kelly's father, Scott, and his wife, Julia, and was looking forward to seeing them both.

Once we arrived at their home, we sat on the back deck, talking and enjoying the late afternoon of the summer day. Of course, none of us was yet conscious of the devastating pain awaiting us. We were unaware that while we were sitting enjoying our cold drinks, laughing and joking, Sean was already dead and the police were at his apartment investigating. Thankfully, we had no knowledge of this, and could still enjoy a small reprieve. We had these last few hours of contentment and peace, until Sean's wife would tell us her devastating news, changing our lives forever.

As Kelly, Liam, and I were driving back home, we realized that she and her father had not secured the cushions of the couch. After seeing one fly away from the bed of the truck, we stopped on the side of the road, only to discover that another cushion was missing too, probably flying away undetected by any of us. We laughed so much, including Liam; even at his young age, he had a great sense of humour. Undoubtedly, he thought of this as yet another adventure with his mother and grandmother.

I mention this because it feels important for me to share the pleasure I experienced that day. I'll always remember the joy in the hours preceding the news of Sean's death. Often, I contrast those warm feelings with the almost unbearable pain I would encounter that night. This time, with Kelly and Liam, filled with happiness, would be one of the last carefree moments I would experience for a very long time.

"When you jump for joy, beware that no one moves the ground from beneath your feet." —*Stanislaw Jerzy Lec*

∞

Robert and I just watched television that night. Around 8:30 p.m., I looked at my emails, noticing one from Sean's wife, asking for our home telephone number. Seeing that she had sent the note about an hour before, I felt some concern. Frequently, I experienced unease when I received an email from my daughter-in-law, as it was usually related to Sean and his drinking. But even though my heart did a little jump, I was confident that whatever the situation was, it would easily be resolved.

Sean had been in recovery for quite a while; it didn't occur to me that he might not be clean. I was feeling secure that all was well in Sean's world, as I had met up with him just two days before. We had spent quite a lot of time together cleaning out a locker where he kept the equipment for his business and we'd had a good time. He looked healthy and happy, which made me feel happy as well. I did not detect any behaviour that would make me think he was drinking or using drugs again.

Sean had celebrated his thirty-fifth birthday a month before. He seemed to be getting his life together, marrying his live-in girlfriend three weeks earlier and moving to an apartment in the Beaches, an area they both loved.

Eager to help with the clean-up of his locker, I picked up a board, puncturing my finger on a nail. Sean immediately stopped what he was doing. Despite my protests, he searched around for his first-aid kit; he poured some peroxide on the cut and put a Band-Aid around my finger. This is how Sean was with me, and I never doubted he loved me very much.

As his mother, I'd had so many problems with Sean because of his addictions. Regularly, I told him that, no matter what, I loved him unconditionally and always would. In return, he trusted me, generally being quite open about his struggles and problems, treating me with respect and affection.

Perhaps I had a tendency to say too much in my discussions with Sean, but, as John Mayer sings in "Say": "It's better to say too much than to never say what you need to say again."

So Sean and I talked a lot about his past, his present, his future—about life, books, and movies. We told each other how much we cared, and enjoyed a mother-son relationship that spilled over into a great friendship, routinely meeting to do things together. We talked once or twice a week, exchanged random emails, and often connected for lunch, dinner, or a coffee at Chapters, with a browse through their books.

Sean was an avid reader who introduced me to the concepts outlined in books by Eckhart Tolle and Warren Buffett, both of whom he greatly admired, obviously for different reasons. In return, I introduced him to my favourites by His Holiness the Dalai Lama and by Dr. Deepak Chopra.

My son was intelligent and skilled at discussing a number of subjects, but he was particularly interested in the financial markets, the economy, world events, and business. Often, I asked his opinion on these matters. Also, because he had his own business, Sean was accustomed to managing people throughout the years, whether staff or sub-contractors. Frequently, I thought if he could get his addictions under control, Sean would become a very successful businessman.

This intelligent, humorous man, with great potential, is the side of Sean I saw customarily. Unfortunately, he was held back by his illness, his dependences.

So I wasn't sure why his wife wanted to talk to me. However, as I mentioned earlier, I wasn't overly concerned and even considered not responding to her request, letting her deal with whatever was going on. Sean was now married. My thoughts were that his wife should interact with him directly rather than asking me to intervene to help get her husband back on track—if such was the problem.

Shortly, I decided to treat her email seriously. And not wanting to disturb Robert, who was watching television, I went upstairs to our bedroom to try to reach her by phone. When my daughter-in-law answered, I had some difficulty understanding what she wanted to discuss. When I asked her what was going on, she responded, "It's about Sean."

I said, "What about Sean?"

She repeated, "It's about Sean."

I was getting somewhat worried, maybe a tad impatient, as I restated, "What about Sean; what is it?"

Silence greeted me.

Becoming increasingly apprehensive, again I asked. She responded, "Well … well … Sean is dead."

I screamed, as I've never screamed before. It was as if a knife had penetrated my heart, shredding it to pieces, cutting through my whole being. The pain was so profound that it was both physical and emotional—the worst torture of my life.

Thank goodness I was in the master bedroom, as I fell, more than sat, on the bed. In the background, I heard my dog, Molly, charging up the stairs. Minutes later Robert burst in. Hysterically, I sobbed that Sean had died, handing the telephone directly to my husband. Remarkably, Sean's wife was still on the line. But as

Robert spoke with her, I was so distraught that I could not follow their conversation.

Later, he told me that our daughter-in-law was incoherent, rambling and repeating, "Sean was in the bathroom, and he is dead." Apparently, whenever Robert asked a question, she'd only repeat "Sean is dead, Sean is dead." Through my tears, I managed to make Robert understand that I was going next door to Kelly's house. Later, Robert told me that he had asked Sean's wife to please call back once she could manage to speak.

When I knocked on Kelly's door, it was after 9:00 p.m., and both she and her husband, Kris, answered. Afterward, my daughter admitted that the instant she glimpsed me through the glass pane of her door, she knew something was dreadfully wrong. Gasping so hard that I could not summon the words to tell her about her brother, grappling for composure, I blurted out, "Sean is dead." Kelly burst into tears. In shock, we held onto each other, soon taking refuge in their living room, where Robert joined us moments later.

Since my husband had been unable to obtain any details from Sean's wife, Kris called the police station responsible for the area where Sean lived. He was told by the investigating detective that drugs had been found near Sean's body, and that he had likely died of an overdose. This information did not penetrate my consciousness. For quite some time, I clung to the thought that Sean had died due to an injury he sustained in his bathroom. My mind seemed unable to accept that drugs were responsible for his death, and I continued to reject this harsh reality, off and on, for two to three weeks.

I was in shock and it seemed as if my brain could not retain certain aspects, but rather rejected them as implausible. Intellectually, I understood, but emotionally the specifics were fluid and continued to elude me. There would be days when I'd wake up, saying to myself, "Sean is dead; he died of a drug overdose." Other mornings, as my eyes opened to this continuing nightmare, I told myself that Sean had died from a fall in his bathroom.

Finally, I asked my son's father, Scott, to send me an email with the details of Sean's death: how he was found, in the bathroom, with a syringe near his body, so that I could refer to it when I was no longer certain of how he had died.

Nature tries to cushion the newly bereaved with shock and denial; while this natural muting helps a little bit, it can be confusing too.

∞

When Robert and I returned home from Kelly's, around 11:30 p.m., I called my sister, Maureen, who shrieked out in shock the minute I told her that her nephew was dead. Since she was unable to speak, her husband came to the telephone. Although I told Bob about Sean's death, I don't remember discussing how he had died. What I do recall is feeling badly, because my sister's birthday would be in thirty minutes; troubled by this, I feared that every year Maureen would link her special day with the traumatic news of Sean's sudden death. During our conversation, my brother-in-law promised they would come to us the next day. I said they shouldn't come. While coping with our tragedy, I could not manage having anyone else in the house—I was not ready for even family, or close friends, to witness my emotional devastation.

Later, after calling my younger sister, Diane, I was so convinced this tragic night would not allow me sleep or any relief from this searing pain that I took two sleeping pills and fitfully drifted into a welcomed oblivion.

Waking the next morning, my very first thought was, "Sean is dead." With waves of despair such that I could barely breathe, it felt as if I was out of control. Robert took me to our medical clinic, where I sobbed unashamedly in their waiting room. A child looked at me curiously, but I could not stop. The receptionist took us to a private office, where the doctor came right away and prescribed lorazepam.

Once I felt calmer, I managed an email to my supervisor and to the team with whom I worked, explaining that Sean had injured himself from a fall in his bathroom and had not woken from his injury. I clung to denial, despite what Kris had discovered the night before. Following this, I spoke with one of my best friends to let her know about Sean. Understandably, she wanted to come to the house, with another friend, to comfort us. Again I refused, unwilling to be seen in such horrible emotional turmoil. She asked if they could at least come over to give us hugs. I had to decline. I could not bear to see anyone.

To this day, I regret rejecting the concerned offers of comfort we received. In retrospect, I sense that having had family and friends present in our home might have provided consolation— not only to us, but also to them. At the time, I didn't perceive it this way—I was only thinking of my own pain and what I felt I could tolerate. Wanting to deal with Sean's death privately, on my own terms, was probably selfish of me. Rather than treating it as a crisis that impacted many people, I was thinking of Sean's loss as my own personal tragedy. The reality was that his death had far-reaching consequences for everyone in his life.

∞

In the subsequent days, I spent all day sitting at the back of our yard, near the fishpond, deeply despondent. On the third day, a white butterfly appeared and started to flutter around me. If I sobbed, it would sweep in next to my chair. It seemed as if the butterfly felt my pain; it became a bit more agitated when my distress increased. Robert also noticed the antics of the butterfly, and we imagined it was Sean telling us that he was all right; he was near.

During the second week, another butterfly joined in; together, they flew past me and around my chair, chasing each other as if to get my attention. If I was enjoying a calm moment, they would fly up higher, near the branches of the trees, but the instant I started to cry, the butterflies flew closer to the ground, directly into my vicinity. Watching them brought such comfort. Every day, as I headed to the pond, they would appear within minutes—even though they had not been there initially. The butterflies remained with me for three whole weeks, and I was sorry when they weren't there anymore.

As I sat near the pond with Robert, we talked about the work Sean had done to try to overcome his addictions: the many meetings, participation in drug and alcohol withdrawal programs, appointments with doctors, psychologists, and much more. We recalled as well that Sean's father, sister, and I had made huge investments of our time, emotions, and finances to help him overcome this malicious disease.

Eventually, I had come to realize that Sean certainly did not want to be an addict; he did not willingly choose this way of living. My son was an addict because our family tree is riddled with members who suffer from alcoholism. It goes back generations, on both sides of the family. Sean was doomed the minute he swallowed his first drink.

Though I didn't love him any less, or any differently, often I hoped he would just stop drinking. His drinking usually led him to taking drugs. Frequently, I reasoned that if he gave up alcohol, his drug issues would be resolved. When Sean and I spoke of this, occasionally I would say, "Sean, all you have to do is not take that first drink, or that first drug, or call someone for help before you take anything."

He would respond, "Mom, you just don't understand addictions. You have to be an addict to understand."

In later years, after having access to expert information and informed literature, I would fully accept that Sean suffered from a debilitating illness, not a lifestyle choice.

∞

Kris and Kelly organized Sean's memorial service, which was a good thing because, frankly, I was unable to. Nearly paralyzed by my pain, I was too busy wondering how to survive Sean's death. I was sobbing constantly. It did not seem possible to cry this much, but the tears just poured down my face.

During these desperate days, I argued with Scott, who wanted to speak at the funeral about Sean's drug use. Strongly, I objected, wanting our son to be remembered for his good qualities. Sean was far more than an addict. My concern was that all of his merits, talents, and abilities would be overshadowed by his dependency on alcohol and drugs.

I sent Scott an email, asking him not to speak of Sean's drug use at the funeral. He responded that he would think about this. After waiting two long, agonizing days, worrying over what his decision would be, I felt as if Scott was leaving me hanging. Now I realize that he may have needed to think it through, and perhaps pray over it.

All I wanted for my son was a celebration of his life, with the focus on his many positive qualities. At last, I asked Kelly to please speak with her father. Thankfully, she was able to obtain his commitment not to mention Sean's addictions when he spoke at the memorial service.

Sean's service was held on June 13, five days after his death. He would be cremated prior to the memorial service, but his father had asked the funeral parlour to first prepare Sean for a viewing by immediate family. In the end, Scott, Julia, and Julia's daughter were the ones who attended the viewing. Kelly refused to go. Although I debated whether or not I could manage this, ultimately I decided that I wanted to remember my son as I had seen him on June 6: very much alive, seemingly happy, and putting a Band-Aid on my finger.

I felt unable to face saying goodbye to Sean in his casket or view him with the life drained out of him. At times I have regretted this decision. On occasion, I have fretted that I missed an opportunity to see my son one last time, to hold him and touch him. Then I rationalize that it's not Sean I would have been holding, but merely his human form. Without his spirit or soul, his body would not contain my dynamic son.

When I walked into the funeral home for the service, I was shocked to see how many people were there. People were even standing at the back. I recognized friends, family, and my colleagues from work, but there were many people I didn't know.

In the five days before the service, all I had done was weep. Finally, on the morning of Sean's memorial, I put together some words and managed to stand up and speak publicly about my son. In my eulogy, I expressed Sean's love of books, his encouragement of me to be more generous (when I had visited an impoverished country prior to his death), his open-heartedness toward poor people, and his reinforcement of my spiritual journey. Then I spoke of his willingness to accompany me to events that, at the time, he might not have been so interested in—such as hearing His Holiness the Dalai Lama speak when His Holiness came to Toronto. I expressed Sean's belief in the middle path, and how he taught me about it. And I let everyone know that he is still with us, even though we are unable to see him.

Having promised myself that I would get through what I had to say about the good side of Sean, I didn't cry when I spoke. When I finished, I was astounded to hear people clapping. At that moment, I wasn't sure why they were applauding, but afterward I suspected they had been supporting my ability to speak at my son's memorial without breaking down.

The breaking down would come later.

Scott kept his word and did not talk about his son's addictions. Kelly spoke of the tumultuous relationship she had had with her brother, and promised that her son would know who his uncle was.

Sean's widow also spoke at his funeral. She was remarkably composed, and I don't remember what she said, except for her reference to her husband's generosity. Never did I see Sean's widow cry over his death—before, during, or in the days following his memorial service, or in the months to follow. After my years of grief work, I recognize that everyone grieves differently. She may have been numbed by shock. But in the depth of my sorrow, this apparent absence of emotion was wrenching for me to witness.

After Sean's service, I spent two more weeks near the pond talking with my husband, who stayed by my side the entire time. I talked, cried, prayed, and cried some more, questioning Robert as to how I would survive. Confiding my fear of the sorrow that loomed ahead of me for years to come, I asked him, "How will I deal with all this heartache?"

Robert listened, held me, and kissed me while reassuring me that I would survive, though he admitted not knowing how. He kept reminding me that, for the time being, I had to live my life one day at a time, one hour at a time, even a minute at a time, if need be, until I started to heal.

What made my path more complicated was that not only had I lost my son, I had also lost a very good friend in Sean. We enjoyed an adult relationship, and truly liked each other's company. I felt doubly touched. Not only had I lost my beloved son, I had to deal with the death of my good friend as well.

When I talked to Sean, I asked him why. That's all I would say: "Why, Sean, why?" I asked this because I was starting to accept that he had died of a drug overdose.

His father had spoken with the coroner, and called me to tell me about this discussion. Although the results of toxicology tests were still pending, the coroner was certain that our son had died of an overdose—one lone, fresh puncture mark had been found on his body.

He said that we would receive the results formally by letter in approximately six months, which would bring us to December. The thought of receiving the cause of Sean's death so close to the first Christmas without him added to my grief. It caused me a lot of stress, but this was something outside of my control. All I could do was hope that the information would be available earlier, so that we could deal with the shock of these findings before the holiday season was upon us.

When asked, I began to disclose that Sean had died of an overdose. Even so, I could not discuss the exact details, as there was much that I still did not know; as well, I seemed powerless to retain those few facts that I did have. To this day, I have some difficulty with the particulars—at times I still need to ask Sean's father about them, or reread the coroner's report.

∞

Returning to work just a month after Sean's death, I was unsure if I was ready. In retrospect, I probably should have taken a longer leave, but I was firmly in denial—not fully processing or accepting our tragedy. I was in search of an escape, and it seems as if I tried to dampen my emotions by putting my son's death on the back burner of my mind.

Although nothing felt as it had before, I had made a decision to show strength in dealing with Sean's death, to move on with my life as well as I could. Even being distracted by work, I did not feel like myself; nonetheless, I kept searching. It seemed as if I was two separate people: the one with the public face, and this other, the one who grieved and mourned, felt such distress, and could not find herself. Feeling I had lost the core of what I was, the "fun-loving, humorous Kathleen," I did not then understand that I would never be the same again. In my heart, I really hoped that, as time went on, the old me would return. Now, after reading so much about grief and mourning, I know this will never happen.

What has happened is that I function normally now—not because I have found myself again, but because I have gotten used to the pain of loss that I feel most days. While I know that there is a hole in my heart that will never be repaired, I have learned to live around my sorrow, enjoying the happy or calm moments that life offers me.

I remember telling people that if I could paint, I would paint a portrait of a naked woman sitting on the ground, curled up in a ball, with an expression of distress on her face—painting her as if she was a puzzle but leaving out one piece: a hole in her heart. This is how I felt and continue to feel. There will always be a piece of me that is missing; this missing part is so significant that it has changed the person I was, and have become.

Constantly, I worried I would take my life, agonizing that I didn't have the strength to live without my son, one of my best friends. Fortunately, I could not leave Robert, whom I love very much, Kelly, or Natalie, my step-daughter, and their respective families. Though they were unaware of the roles they played, the love that I had for each and every one of them kept me alive. My faith also kept me going. When I felt like dying, I would turn to God and to my guardian angel, asking them to help, reverting to my Catholic background.

The times when I was in a lot of trouble, crying hysterically and in such emotional agony, which I felt helpless to bear, I would ask—no, beg, "God, please, please, send hundreds, even thousands, of angels to my rescue. Send them to help carry me until my pain has abated." I know that my prayers were heard because I felt so much better when I prayed to God and requested His help in getting me through my anguish.

∞

Despite my broken heart, eventually I sensed that I was starting to progress. Often, I would analyze my changing behaviour—a review of my state of mind as to where I had been and where I was now. I recalled how much I had wept, literally from morning to night, immediately following Sean's death, and then just three-quarters of the day in the preceding weeks. About a month later, I was breaking down for half a day. Certainly it was still a lot, and some nights I sobbed so much that Robert held me until I was able to calm down. But deep down I was starting to feel hopeful, believing I would survive and continue to live my life, albeit a life without Sean. My return to work after only a one-month absence, although a bit too soon, kept me more focussed. When I did cry, mostly it was at the end of my workday.

By August, I was falling apart only about a quarter of the day, some days more, some days less, depending on what my thoughts were or the emotional strength I possessed on a particular day. Grieving is like that. It's up and down, and so many other factors can enter into how one feels on a certain day.

The first day that I did not weep at all, I was immensely proud that I had managed through a whole day; I felt sure this accomplishment boded better days ahead. In reality, I had only the one good day and spent the next three making up for it.

Still, as the months progressed, I was noticing and mentally charting these little improvements: a day without tears, a discussion about Sean without a total meltdown, being able to manage a visit with two of Sean's friends without an emotional collapse.

Yes, I was progressing.

Life was changing for me. The people from whom I had expected to receive enormous support did not come through. Of course, I had rejected many offers of encouragement in the day or two following Sean's death, and people did not realize how much I needed them now—now that my hysteria had somewhat abated. Also, I think that some did not know what to say, or how to express their feelings about Sean's death. If anything, many seemed to avoid asking about my son—as if they wanted me to move on very quickly and put his loss behind me as soon as possible.

Although I needed my old friends, I didn't know how to ask for their help. I had never been one to look for assistance; this was a new role for me. In the end, most of my friends, and some family members, did not come through for me. Perhaps they were doing their own grieving and wanted to mourn Sean privately.

Eventually, I mourned more naturally and with less craziness—for lack of a better word—and because of this I didn't feel as ashamed of my pain. It's odd to use the word "shame" in the same sentence as "pain," but this is how I felt. Ashamed of being such an emotional mess, I did not realize (back then) that tears of loss are not a sign of weakness, or that random bursts of grief are a normal part of mourning.

Sometimes, driving in the truck with Robert—he would be chatting about something completely unrelated to Sean—the realization would hit me full-force: "My son actually is dead," and the tears would start pouring. My husband would pull over and park on the side of the road to hold me until I could get myself under control. I am certain that many people misinterpreted my tears, thinking that we were having a disagreement, while essentially Robert was my earth angel, making sure that I recovered to the extent that I could and would. Needless to say, he is my number one.

∞

Another difficulty was all the restaurants and places that Sean and I had visited together, especially Chapters. Two months after his death, on August 8, I gathered my strength to go there on my own. I knew I had to take this step. It felt like visiting the store without Sean would be a sort of victory over my grief.

As I got out of my truck and walked through the parking lot, already I was shaking. I was teary-eyed as I entered the front door. It was impossible to believe that I was walking into Chapters without Sean by my side; it was even worse knowing that he would never walk in with me again. Entering the aisle that held books about the afterlife, I became so distraught that I started to sob, not caring who saw or heard that I was upset in public. After all, I had cried just about everywhere anyway; what was one more store?

A woman browsing one aisle over must have overheard. She came around the corner asking if she could help and introduced herself as Paula Connor. Pouring my heart out to this stranger, I told her about Sean's death, and how we used to come to Chapters together. It turned out that she was quite knowledgeable about books on life after death. She suggested several for me to read. When I asked for a recommendation of the best ones to purchase, she said to buy the books that spoke to me from the shelf, and that I would know which ones they were. This stranger stood by my side in the bookstore aisle, talking with me about Sean and the afterlife. She reminded me that my son was still with me. She listened. My emotional state did not seem to make her uncomfortable in any way. After about an hour, we went our separate ways. To this day, I am thankful to this woman named Paula Connor, who showed such compassion to a complete stranger.

Other people really surprised me too. A woman at work, Lorraine Young, who worked in another division of the organization, started to send emails of encouragement. Lorraine was not even one of my colleagues; she worked in an area completely unrelated to my work. She had worked with my daughter, and I knew her through Kelly. I welcomed her emails and poured my heart out to her, sharing the depths of my pain. She never seemed to tire of my communications, often initiating the notes, resulting in a series of exchanges to discuss Sean's death and my grief. Her words and thoughts on life after death always raised my spirits.

On occasion, I would sit at my computer, beginning with words to the effect, "Today is a bad day, Lorraine." Always, I received a return note that same day, often within minutes, with words of compassion and encouragement to get me through my day. I found it much easier to express my deepest feelings to her than to my family or close friends. She opened a door for me through which I could express the depth of my despair.

Although Lorraine valued me and expressed warm compassion, we hadn't had enough time to forge a long friendship where she would personally be affected by the full depths of my agony. Whereas my family was immersed deeply in my grief and in their own—suffering right alongside me—perhaps Lorraine held some emotional space, which was very helpful to her and to me. She never told me what to do, or how I should feel. Rather, Lorraine would respond that she could not understand what I was going through, not having lost a child, but that the mere thought of it filled her with fear. Saying that she would always be there when I needed her, she was incredible, another of my earth angels.

Almost immediately following Sean's death, my sister Diane, who lives several hundred kilometres away, started to send me emails. Also, it seemed in those first few months as if she called me every day. Diane understood how completely devastated I was. She would listen as I opened my heart, telling her how much sadness I was feeling, how very much I missed my son. At the end of our discussions, she often would say, "Don't cry, Kathleen, I'll call tomorrow." My sister let me know that she was praying for me and had asked her guardian angel to help me—that I needed her guardian much more than she did at this time.

Diane has a calm voice, and uses such gentle words. I've never heard her utter a harsh response. She has a good soul, this younger sister of mine. Always, she knew how I was feeling and found the right assurances to bring more peace and calm into my life. It was Diane, the little earth angel she is, who taught me to ask for help from angels. She knew I prayed to God a lot, but said that I should start praying to angels too and sent me a book that she used as a reference for her life. This guide meant a lot to Diane; she referred to it frequently, and for her to willingly part with it demonstrated how much she loved me.

Many emails from family, friends, and colleagues touched my heart. It was then that I understood for certain that people were thinking of me, and praying for Sean, my family, and me. These notes were a comfort when, at times, I would wake up wondering how to get through another day. I thank all these people deeply. They know who they are.

∞

In early December, we received the coroner's report. Sean's cause of death was listed as acute fentanyl toxicity. So indeed he had died of an overdose, using a drug that I had never heard of before. Fentanyl, a powerful synthetic opiate, is much more potent than morphine. It is used to treat severe pain, and in palliative care. It can be purchased on the street, where there have been many deaths associated with its abuse. In addition to fentanyl, Sean had methadone, morphine, and alcohol in his system. Overwhelmed, I could not rationalize how normal my son had looked on June 6, such a short time before his death.

Although I was aware Sean was on a methadone program, I had no idea, nor was it obvious, that he was using illegal drugs and drinking again. How could I have been so blind? Had Sean deceived me to this extent? Did I know my son so little that I could not detect signs of drug abuse? I decided to call the coroner, who told me that it was quite possible Sean had just then resumed his drug use, as the autopsy had revealed only one puncture mark on his body.

The coroner explained that oftentimes addicts who are in recovery and start using drugs again return to the dosage at which they left off. This is just too much for the heart. He said Sean's death would have been very quick. More than likely, he would have fallen asleep; his heart would simply have stopped. Having often feared that my son might die through violence due to his lifestyle, the coroner's words brought me some measure of comfort.

At least Sean had not suffered. But I was angry that he had left us in such a state of misery, and I would spend quite some time working on forgiving him for dying in such a negligent way. My son was savvy and knew the risks he incurred. As a matter of fact, he had spoken, on occasion, about how concerned he was that his drug use might lead to his death.

∞

Sean suffered from an illness—an addiction that he had made several significant efforts to overcome. Even though I tried to look at his death as the result of a disease, his loss still caused a lot of sorrow; as I mentioned, I really had to work hard on forgiving him.

Christmas 2012 was fast approaching and, dreading this first one without Sean, I was breaking down more often. As someone who follows a Buddhist way of living, I do not personally celebrate Christmas, but I do buy presents for my family and friends, and partake of their Christmas meal.

In the weeks prior to December 25, I experienced a lot of turmoil as I went into stores to shop for family and friends. When some item or other would catch my eye, I would think, "Oh, Sean will love that," but then I'd remember that I would not be buying any gifts for Sean. It tore me apart; I'd break down wherever I was, crying my heart out thinking of Christmas without him.

It was an extremely difficult time. Then, miraculously, I was blessed. During a meditation in mid-December, I found myself walking along a path in a forest. In my meditation, Sean suddenly appeared, walking beside me. When I saw him next to me, I became very emotional.

He spoke softly, saying, "Mom, I want you to know that I have moved on where I am and also I am very busy. I would like you to move on too."

As Sean finished speaking, we came to a fork in the path; he took one path while I stayed on mine. As I turned to look toward Sean, he was looking back at me. He gave me a little wave and then turned his back and kept on walking. I gasped as I came out of my meditation. Although I was still weepy, I experienced tremendous relief in perceiving that Sean had accepted his situation. He was moving on and wanted me to do the same. More at peace, I started to work harder to regain my emotional grounding.

On December 22, we placed Sean's ashes in a columbarium. Sean's widow did not participate. She claimed that her employer would not give her the time off work. While I wondered about this at the time, and even found it rather appalling that Sean's widow did not attend her husband's internment, today it does not matter to me. I also found it strange that she did not ask for her husband's ashes after the memorial service, but rather deferred to me when I took them from the funeral director. For this, I always will be grateful to her because in the end, as his wife, she probably could have insisted on receiving Sean's ashes. Then I would have lost track of my son's remains.

∞

In February of 2013, when I felt like I was progressing, the ground fell out from under me when Sean's father emailed me a copy of a report called the Coroner's Investigative Statement. We had had no idea that this was forthcoming. Upon reading it, I discovered that my daughter-in-law's version of the events surrounding Sean's death (as she had explained them to me) did not correspond to that contained in the Coroner's Investigative Statement.

This short, factual report indicated that Sean's wife had reported that she last saw Sean around 1:30 p.m., when he arrived home, went into the bathroom, and locked the door. At 2:00 p.m., unable to get a response from Sean, she left and went to a coffee shop to use their facilities. When she returned home (the time was not stated), she tried again to get a response from Sean. At 4:00 p.m., believing he was in medical distress, she used a hammer and screwdriver to create a hole in the bathroom door in order to unlock the door. After gaining access, she found Sean unresponsive. She attempted resuscitation and called 9-1-1 at 5:00 p.m. The emergency services arrived at 5:09 p.m.

This was a very different version of events than the one she had previously told me. In the months following Sean's death, I had discussed the circumstances with my daughter-in-law. She had said that on the day of his death, Sean had come home around 1:00 p.m. She relayed that he did not look very well; he was ill and sweating when he went into the washroom. Around 1:30 p.m., realizing that she had not heard anything from Sean, she had called out to him. He did not respond. Then she told me that she had seen his black hair "poking out from under the door of the bathroom" and had started looking for the bathroom key. She said she looked for about twenty minutes, and then spent another fifteen to twenty minutes making a hole in the door with some tools. When she saw Sean slumped over, she said that she called 9-1-1.

Hearing this original story, I had agonized over the fact that she had not immediately called the emergency services when Sean did not respond to her. For months, I had worked hard on forgiving her for what seemed to me to be a serious lapse in judgement, and I am sincere in saying that I had.

The Coroner's Investigative Statement was a game changer. The circumstances of Sean's death were worse than I had imagined. For one thing, it appeared that our daughter-in-law had lied to us. This disturbed me profoundly. Also, I was appalled that she had left the house, and her husband, under these conditions. Various scenarios played themselves out in my mind. What if she had called emergency services immediately when Sean did not answer her? Seeing Sean's hair "poking out from underneath the door," why hadn't she realized that he was in serious distress? What if she had sought help from a neighbour?

Then I recalled that, shortly after my son's death, I had spoken with one of his workers, who told me he had gone to pick up Sean around 2:00 p.m. on June 8. His wife had answered their door and told him that Sean would be out shortly. When he never appeared, the worker finally left. At the time, this discussion did not seem significant. Now, I wondered why my daughter-in-law had not taken advantage of the worker's presence to tell him about the situation developing with her husband—that he was in the washroom and not responding.

Since I still had Sean's cell phone, I decided to check the text messages he had sent and received on the day of his death. From 2:11 p.m. to 2:36 p.m., his wife had sent Sean six text messages, but there were no answers from him. In one of the messages, at 2:36 p.m., she informed Sean that the worker who had been waiting for him had left.

In the end, it looks as if our daughter-in-law lied to us and to the police. She told them she left the house at 2:00 p.m., when there she was still texting Sean at 2:36 p.m. It is feasible one might under/overestimate the time, especially with such stressful conditions. However, it is difficult to believe she misjudged her time of departure by thirty-six minutes. In addition, my daughter-in-law did not inform the police about Sean's worker coming to her door during the crisis. Nor did she disclose that she had not told this worker that Sean had looked ill when he went into the bathroom and that he was not responding to her.

This new information caused tremendous emotional turmoil for us. Robert and I, along with Scott and Julia, met with the detective who had investigated Sean's death. In essence, we were told that, no matter what, Sean's wife had met her due diligence under Canadian law by calling 9-1-1, albeit a few hours later and after Sean's death. This additional information about her timeline or her failure to report that a worker had come to the door was of no interest to the detective. We realized nothing further would be gained from our interaction with the police.

Although I cannot know for certain, sometimes today I question if a possibility exists that my daughter-in-law failed to recognize Sean's dire and imminent peril. Back then, the inconsistencies and half-truths continually magnified the horror of my son's tragic death, robbing me of any strength to speculate further.

An emotional tailspin ensued. I had to take time off work and spent the next five months in starting-over mode. Even with my anguish over Sean's death, I began to realize that I had been in a great deal of denial. Now I decided to deal with my grief in a healthier way.

At the advice of my family doctor, I did what I should have done already in the year following Sean's death: I sought out a therapist. This was the best thing I could have done, as this second year was proving to be a tough one for me. Fortunately, I found the right therapist and, because of this, I faced the fact that Sean was dead, accepted that he was not coming back, and recognized that I would never see him again in this life.

In addition, my doctor was of immense support during this period. We had regular appointments: weekly, initially, then bi-weekly, and then monthly as I progressed. He was someone with whom I could speak candidly, disclosing all the thoughts that were tormenting me. He really helped, and I will be forever grateful to this doctor for lending me his full support.

∞

In May 2013, once more I became a regular visitor at the Bereaved Families of Ontario-York Region (BFOYR) office. During the first month following Sean's death, I had received enormous encouragement from this association. But, clearly, in those early days I was not yet ready to do my grief work. Afterwards, for quite some time, I did not communicate further with BFOYR. However, once I fully comprehended that I had been in denial about Sean's death for close to a year, I quickly reconnected with them. A one-on-one interview was arranged with a volunteer bereavement facilitator. She helped me appreciate the grief work I had accomplished throughout the past year. As well, she gently pointed out that much of my work in understanding my bereavement still lay ahead for me. This was a turning-point meeting, giving me the impetus that propelled me forward to make a conscious decision to work through my grief in the face of the pain that awaited me.

This discussion also helped me absorb that all of my family members were grieving, each one at his or her own pace. As well, suggestions were made, such as participating in support sessions (which I did) and reading and/or journaling. At this point, I was reading again and had started to borrow from the library, in due time reading close to twenty books on bereavement. These narratives, though different from one another, really helped me understand the grieving process. As I read the various stories, I started to see that grief was a journey. I identified with the authors, thinking to myself, "Yes, I went through this," or "No, I haven't experienced that."

In the end, these books on loss and healing offered a tremendous hope that I could heal. They also helped me realize that while I would never be the same person again, I could still have a life—a life that was worthwhile, and one that included joy and purpose as well.

∞

Through dealing with my anger at Sean, I have forgiven him for dying and for the heartache he caused our family. Also, I have worked hard on my anger at my daughter-in-law and have forgiven her too, although I choose not to have a relationship with her. The hardest part of this decision is that she is someone who has many memories of life with Sean, having spent several years with him. She could be a tremendous source of stories when I want to reminisce about my son.

During my continuing journey, I have learned that we do not know how anyone, including ourselves, will react in an emergency, or later to grief and despair. During some of the interactions by phone and in person, our daughter-in-law likely was in shock.

Regrettably, there is much I will never know, many things I struggle to understand, and others I have not managed to accept. Still, I do see that on her wedding day, my daughter-in-law could not have envisioned that in just three weeks she would be a widow. For the hopeful promises of new beginnings never ever to be fulfilled, I am everlastingly sorry for us all.

My heart is starting to accept that hurting us was not our daughter-in-law's intent; nonetheless, the conflicting, painful discrepancies in her stories resulted in deep distress for us all. So although forgiveness has come, I cannot manage a bond with the person who appeared to abandon Sean to his fate. Yes, my son played a very significant and principal role in his own demise. But his wife's apparent negligence in failing to come to his immediate aid, sadly, holds me back from seeking a relationship with her.

∞

In May 2014, one month prior to the second anniversary of Sean's death, shocking new information arrived for me to assimilate. One of Sean's friends, from whom I had not heard since my son's death, telephoned me. During our discussion, he divulged that in the week preceding his death, Sean had mentioned suicide to him twice; the first time he had said that he wanted to take the easy way out, the second time that he was thinking of ending it. His friend thought this was only talk. After his friend provided him with a response indicating the pain that his death would cause our family, Sean spoke of it no further to him.

From the outset, I had suspected that there was a possibility my son might have taken his own life. When I expressed these thoughts to my family or to my friends, none agreed. My family's argument was that if Sean had committed suicide, he would have—at the very least—left a note to explain his actions, because of our close relationship. Afterwards, I seldom revealed these concerns, except in discussions with Robert; just the same, I continued to ponder whether Sean might have committed suicide. He was too astute, where drugs were concerned, to have used so many together while expecting to survive the combinations and the doses he took.

Though I will never know for sure whether Sean died of an accidental drug overdose or at his own hand, it does not change my feelings about him or about his death. He was very ill. When I feel deep pain at his loss, I remind myself that he was hurting in so many ways. Now, I can somehow fathom the action he may have taken to end his anguish—Sean was tormented for most of his youth and adulthood by his addictions—if this, in fact, is what happened. After watching my son's suffering, I cannot stay angry at him for making a decision to end it all. I can only love him, forgive him, and remember all of our good times together, because there were many good times for him and me. This is what I will continue to focus on, as I have done for the last several years.

∞

Sean's father and his wife, and my husband and I, always celebrate the special occasions concerning Sean by releasing balloons. We have dedicated a garden to him and planted a rose bush in his honour. I visit my son regularly at the cemetery, where I think of him and pray for him. Speaking with him daily, sometimes I still cry, but more and more I don't. When I see a Beetle car, I even play punch buggy with Sean, punching the air, because we used to play that game together. I laugh as I do this, trying to have positive happy memories of my son and not just mourn him.

Sean is forever enmeshed in the fabric of my heart and in our memories as a family. He is our son, brother, uncle, and brother-in-law. He was a source of love and friendship—it is important to continue to talk about him and to include him.

I am honest in my memories. Although I laugh at his pranks, I speak seriously of Sean's addictions. Deeply, I wish that we could have been successful in helping him overcome this terrible illness. I consistently tried whatever I could, following the advice provided by doctors and specialists.

I forgive myself for not always doing the right thing, and for sometimes doing the wrong thing. I have slowly pardoned myself for not having understood addiction as an illness until much later in my life, only grasping it more fully when chemical and alcohol dependencies were better recognized by the general public, and I had access to the technology to educate myself.

∞

Looking back at the time that has passed, I am amazed at my journey and by the people I have met along the way. When my path began on the day of Sean's death, I cried every minute of every day, struggling to survive and doubting that I could. Today, I can speak about Sean without too much drama, and actually play punch buggy with him.

Sean still has an email account; occasionally, I send him an email to tell him how I miss him, love him, and how life is going with the family—as if he doesn't know. I like having this secret relationship with him. Sometimes when I see a really funny joke I'll send it to him, knowing that he would have loved it and that we would have laughed. It is those memories, and the fierce love that I have for him, which will forever keep Sean alive in my life. For some, this may seem somewhat dysfunctional, but for me, right now, it just makes me happy. Sometimes I'm actually giggling as I write, wondering what some people might think.

Truly, I have found some happiness again. Of course, there is still a hole in my heart. In many ways, it will always be there. Never will I be the person I once was, but I feel now even through my sadness and pain that I am a better person for having lost Sean. For you who may be newly bereaved, please don't feel angry when you read those words. What I mean is that I have genuinely grown since Sean's death. Today, I have more patience, more gentleness, and more compassion toward people. I don't sweat the small stuff so much. With all my heart, I would prefer to have Sean back in my life, but since I cannot have my beloved son here with me, I choose to live a life that honours him.

In August 2013, I took early retirement from work to spend most of my time with my husband, my family, and friends old and new. While I've forgiven my old friends for sometimes not "understanding" or "being there," I also appreciate my new friends for their support.

Recently, I finished classes at BFOYR; I am qualified as a Volunteer Bereavement Facilitator. I love this work. It is painful at times, but I feel that I am helping others in their recovery, making a contribution again. It is my turn now to help in the same manner that I was helped. It is my turn to give back, taking our family's horrible, tragic life experience and turning it into something that makes sense to me.

My son's tragic death has taught me so much. Sean, you were always the one to move me forward, and your aching absence has forced me to grow. For what your life and love have taught me, I am grateful—I am so thankful for you, Sean.

∞

My days have continued to bring unexpected life-changing events for me and my family—as time often does for many of us. As mentioned, in August 2013 I took early retirement. Robert decided to join me. We had so many plans: we spoke of travelling, camping, visiting family and friends, house-finishing projects, and doing absolutely nothing. Still, all was not well. Robert was feeling ill and did not look healthy. His breathing was off. I was very worried and he was as well. Over Thanksgiving 2013, Robert had so many health issues that he was hospitalized, and after an MRI, we were told that he had stage IV lung cancer. The oncologist said that my husband had four to eighteen months to live. We looked at each other like deer caught in the headlights. How could this be? This could *not* be possible. I could not fathom losing my number-one earth angel. Would God give us another overwhelming challenge so soon after Sean's death?

Robert and I talked, and he told me that he wanted to die at home. He loved our home so much; this is where he was most comfortable and wanted to spend the remainder of his life. I assured him that I would do my utmost to make his wish come true, and I did. Following a very brave struggle with his cancer, my dear Robert died at home on January 4, 2015.

Now, sadly, I'm back fully to my grieving. But I have learned so much from my son's death that when I experience any specific feeling, I think to myself, "Oh, yes, I remember that anger" or "I remember that guilt." While continuing to work on my grief, I write, participate in hopeful art projects, and have resumed my therapy, which offers a healing place to share my true feelings.

The sorrow of Robert's death has made it even more pressing and meaningful for me to help others with their losses when I'm requested to do so. In these ways and more, I continue to choose life—for all those who love me, for all who have passed, and for myself as well—because I have much to accomplish in my remaining years.

Life without Robert is difficult. And, as you can imagine, I miss him dearly. But there is no need to go there; you, the reader, and I, the writer, have experienced the despair of bereavement. We are well aware of the deep pain of such significant losses. There is no need for words anymore.

Chapter Seven

Brenda's Story

Susan Massey

Brenda Ann Healey:
February 13, 1981–March 8, 2008

"Do not boast about tomorrow
For you do not know what
a day may bring."
—*Proverbs 27:1*

Brenda's Story

I was enjoying my Saturday morning sleep-in. In my dream I hear a ringing, but I cannot find the phone; it just keeps ringing and ringing. My son comes into the bedroom and says, "Nana's on the line, and it sounds like something is wrong."

When I speak to my mom, I can hear the sheer panic in her voice and immediately I ask her, "What's wrong?" She tells me that my sister Brenda is missing. She didn't come home from work last night.

I grew incensed. "What do you mean that she didn't come home? Why didn't you call me?"

She said, "Susan, I have been calling you for hours."

The time is 8:00 a.m. My parents were on their way to the police station in Sutton. My mom said she would call me as soon as she had any new information. I immediately called my sister Teresa. In shock, all she could say is that she would pack up her things and get her newborn daughter ready for the drive to Newmarket.

Over the next two-and-a-half hours, there were so many calls between me, my mom, and my sister—far too numerous to remember details. We were sharing our worry, praying urgently, and checking in to see if anyone knew anything at all.

Then I phoned Brenda's boyfriend, Scott, who told me that he and their friends had been looking for Brenda all night long. He had reported her missing to the police, searched the hospitals, and even gone to her work. Brenda was nowhere to be found. He was heading back to Sutton to see if he could find her there. I asked Scott if my husband should go with him in case he needed help. He came and picked up my husband.

The time is 10:30 a.m.

My mom called to say that she and my dad were at the police station, waiting for the detectives to arrive and interview them. Mom said that all along the roads they had driven, they'd searched the ditches to see if perhaps Brenda was involved in a car crash and had slid off the road. They had spotted nothing unusual, but the weather was so awful. It was the biggest snow storm in fifty years.

Teresa and her family arrived. I recall my son trying to be so positive, telling me that everything was going to be okay.

I said to him, "This is not going to end well."

Knowing something was extremely wrong, I still had no idea what we were in for. Although I could feel a foreboding in the pit of my stomach, all the while I was praying to God to let her be okay—to let her come home.

Every minute felt like an hour; time moved so slowly. The lack of information was frustrating, and there were too many emotions at once.

The time was 12:08 p.m., on Saturday, March 8, 2008, when my husband called and said, "Oh Sue, I am so very sorry—the police have found Brenda, and she is dead."

This was far beyond my powers to believe. Instantly I was immersed in an ice-cold shock, while at the same time blanketed in welcomed denial. It felt as if I was in a movie.

Though I don't recall much of this phone call, I do remember looking at Teresa and seeing a hurt on her face I will never forget. My husband was on his way home with my parents. In the midst of this devastating news, we needed to huddle together and try our best to comfort each other.

It seemed Brenda had gone to pick up her paycheque from her co-worker, Stephen Daniels, who was house-sitting because his friend was in the hospital. It was there, in that house, where Brenda had been discovered, drowned in the bathtub. The accused, Daniels, had committed suicide—at 3:03 a.m., Daniels lay down in front of a train.

My parents arrived home and my sister and I went over to their house. It was the longest walk ever. As we burst through the door, each of us grabbed on tightly to the others. As I reached my dad, he just fell into my arms. For a split second he was completely limp, as if every speck of life had been sucked right out of him. It is an image that remains embedded in my mind. Together as a family, we cried and cried for this horrific loss of our beloved Brenda.

During those moments we agreed that Daniels had already taken far too much from our family. We would allow him to take no more!

My mother said, "Thank God we get to bring Brenda home." In that second, while not yet realizing it, I chose to live.

Family and friends arrived at my parents' home the following day. My husband's parents came to stay with us. My mother-in-law kept us fed and watched our children so that we could be with my parents. Neighbours and the community sent food to help us out. Brenda had always shopped at a particular boutique called Lemon Berry; they opened their store to us and donated a special outfit for Brenda.

The support surrounding us was both loving and overwhelming. It gave us tremendous comfort to see how cherished Brenda was and to feel the positive impact she'd had on so many people. Brenda Ann Healey was a daughter, a sister, an aunt, a girlfriend, a cousin, a friend. And she so much loved all of us.

Brenda was an animal lover who exuded only goodness and kindness. She was always there to lend a hand, share a laugh, or shed a tear with those she loved. My sister was not afraid to try new things and seek new experiences in life; I admired her for this. At every stage of her life, people remembered Brenda for her hardy laugh and her beautiful smile—a smile that would light up a whole room.

Immediately everything started to happen.

The next few days were filled with such difficult tasks ... police meetings, interviews, funeral arrangements, and Brenda's autopsy. Then there was the shocking requirement to identify Brenda's body. In the meantime, we continued to pray that it was not her in the morgue—please! It is hard to inch forward when you are in a state of denial and shock, continually thinking, "This is a mistake," "This cannot be happening!" and "They have found the wrong person."

My brain circled in a loop—I kept calling Brenda's cell phone, hoping against hope that she would pick up. It felt as if she was going to walk in the door any minute, but she did not.

Funeral arrangements were made. Once they were in place, we headed to the coroner's office to identify Brenda. As we left the funeral home, we received a call informing us that the accused, Stephen Daniels, had been convicted for assault in 1999. He had just finished his probation when Brenda started her job with the same company where he was working for his friend.

How could this be allowed to happen? Why?

Everything was getting worse. I felt as if this nightmare must be taking place for another unfortunate family, not for us. Nothing felt real.

∞

The rules of the coroner's office were that only one person could attend. They advised us not to bring a group, but there was no way I was letting my parents go alone. As we waited for the coroner to come out of his office, I looked at my dad and said, "Please let me do this for you?" He bravely said that he was fine, which I felt was his shock talking. I was so worried that identifying his little girl would kill him. He would simply die of a broken heart. Finally Dad agreed to let me go. I truly thought that I was doing something helpful. Nevertheless, I have guilt for taking this moment from him. Later I would worry, "Perhaps I should have encouraged him to identify Brenda." I struggle with this. Embracing the guilt, I have written about it, apologized to my dad, and tried to let it go, but every now and then it sneaks back in.

As I entered that cold, stark morgue with the coroner and the detective, over and to the left was my sister. Brenda was on a gurney, wrapped in a white sheet—only her face was exposed.

The detective asked me, "Is this Brenda?"

I answered, "Yes."

They allowed me a few moments with my baby sister. Oh, how I sobbed. Apologizing to Brenda for this happening and for not protecting her, I gave her a kiss from all of us and told her how much we loved her.

It broke my heart to leave her there. But in a strange way, she looked peaceful. Somehow she didn't look as if she had suffered. In that precious moment, this serene feeling from Brenda lent me a miniscule relief.

As I left the morgue to return to my parents, the coroner looked at me, and with little apparent empathy he said, "Okay, pull it together." Perhaps I was out of control, and possibly he was thinking of my mom and dad. I do not know. As we joined my parents, the coroner spent a few minutes talking to us about Brenda's death. It was excruciating.

He said the cause of death was drowning, but there had been no fight for her life and he felt that maybe she had been drugged. We would have to wait for the toxicology and autopsy reports to come back, which would take nine months. He gave his condolences and left.

There was far too much for us to take in, understand, or even hear. How would we survive? The words I had spoken earlier, about not allowing Brenda's killer to take any more from me or my family, felt much too big to be fulfilled.

On the day of Brenda's funeral, it was bitterly cold and cloudy. The media were set up across the street from the church. The church was crammed full, standing room only. There must have been over eight hundred people in attendance. I was a pallbearer for my sister and remember walking into the church, seeing the people, hearing the poignant hymn "Amazing Grace," and then truly feeling as if I was floating to the front pew.

Though I don't remember a thing about the service, I do recall as clear as day that during Brenda's eulogy—through a small window, way up in the church and far to the right—the sun came pouring in. Then I knew my sister was letting us know she was with us.

Today I understand that my expectations were unrealistic, but during those early days of grief I waited for relief to come. This heavy weight on my shoulders and on my heart would not go away—would not ease. I hoped that as I moved beyond the processes of identifying Brenda, enduring her funeral, and discovering what had happened to my sister, the all-pervasive intensity of my loss and the concentration of my pain would, ever so slowly, ease a tiny bit—but it did not.

∞

Looking back, I realize I was in survivor mode. I was not living—I merely existed. But I needed to live; there was no choice. I had two children and a husband who depended on me. I could not give my family any more pain, and needed to assure my children that somehow, day by day, we were going to be okay. I also wanted to live for my parents; it was crucial for them to trust that, as a family, we were going to make it. Giving up was not an option. Brenda would want us to live.

The pain was another story … weeks had gone by, and I was not eating or sleeping. Emotionally shattered, I convinced myself to go to the doctor. Asking for help is not easy for me. Never before in my life had I felt so weak. I was broken. The doctor prescribed some medication to aid with sleep and anxiety. I had never needed this kind of medication before; needing it now caused me to feel I had failed. Badly, I needed to sleep, and the medication helped with this, but I remained depleted.

I was hoping so much for my heartache to mend, but sadly there was no magic pill for that. The doctor asked if I felt as if I was going to harm myself. Being honest with him, I said, "Yes, and I have a plan." But would I carry it out? No. Why not? … I couldn't, because of my children, my husband, and all of my family. For me, reaching out for help was also making a choice for life, but how could I find help and where?

As it turned out, Victim Services of York Region was the first group that reached out to our family. Yet it was difficult to let strangers into our world and allow them to help us. My trust and security were compromised but, eventually, I relented. Victim Quick Response was made available to us. This program offered us support, counselling, and therapy contacts. It was a short-term program, but certainly it pointed me in the right direction. It makes me proud to say that my relationship with Victim Services flourished, and later they partnered with us to start our homicide support group.

Then I attended therapy with a psychologist: a kind, caring, and compassionate woman who walked me through the darkest days of my life. My therapy with her continued for twenty-four months, but I needed more. I needed to meet other people who had gone through similar anguish; I required some personal assurance that I was going to make it through. With this in mind, I contacted a Distress Centre that offered a homicide support group. I was put on the waiting list for the next session, and this took eighteen long months. Eventually, this is where I met five survivors and it was a very helpful experience for me. Finally, I was in a place where people understood how I felt. The group lasted for eight weeks, and it was sad when the time came for it to end.

My doctor recommended that I see a psychiatrist to help manage my medication and offer extra support. As it turned out, this was not a good experience for me, and it did not last long. This psychiatrist demonstrated a complete lack of compassion and empathy. Unfortunately, he had no interest in helping me. Very shortly, I made sure that he knew how I felt and did not return.

In the meantime, I searched the libraries for books that I hoped would help get me through the days. I read so much that I'm not sure how much I retained; nevertheless, these words gave me validation and comfort. There was one book in particular that helped immensely: *A Grief Like No Other,* written by Kathleen O'Hara.

Then there was journaling, which became a huge part of me in the first three years following Brenda's death. As often as possible I wrote, sometimes during the day and then before bed whenever I could. I made this a quiet time for myself; I wrote about my day, how I felt, anything that came to mind, no matter how difficult. As well, I spent hours on the computer searching for groups and information on homicide—anything to help me, to help us.

Information is power, and I needed to empower myself in the best way I could.

∞

My choice to live unfolded to be a lot of hard work. It took years for me to get to a good place, and I never seemed to know how long that good place would last.

The official investigations went on for the ten months or so following Brenda's death. We continued to go to meetings with the police, where little bits of information would be released. Slowly we were able to piece together what had happened. Personally, I needed to know every single detail, as this was the only way I could begin to process our nightmare. At every meeting I would ask lots of questions and make copious notes, knowing that otherwise I would forget everything. Another casualty of grief—albeit temporary—is memory.

Brenda went to work and never came home. What we learned from the investigation—some of which we already knew—is that Brenda had gone to pick up her paycheque, a common practice in this company. To do so, she had gone to her co-worker's friend's house. A struggle took place in this home, and Brenda was murdered.

Through the media we found out that the alleged killer, Stephen Daniels, had a past criminal record: in 1999 he was charged with attempted murder and had been allowed (successfully) to plea bargain for assault. Daniels was sentenced to two years in jail. He served seven months, then took an anger management course and was released. A friend took him in, and gave him a job and a place to live. His job was at the same company where Brenda worked. At no time was Brenda told of his past, and yet Daniels was left in charge of managing my sister. He was obsessed with her. Brenda was harassed without recognizing the reality of what was happening or the danger of it.

I was having such a hard time accepting the horror of what had happened to Brenda. No matter how I tried to process this information, I could not comprehend that one person would force this fatal brutality upon another human being, especially my sister. Strongly, I felt that someone had to be accountable for allowing this to happen. Then and there, I made a promise that for the rest of my life I would do whatever I could to help survivors of homicide—again choosing to live fully.

Brenda's death devastated not only our immediate family but our extended family as well; she had aunts, uncles, and cousins who loved her dearly. Family memories sometimes centered on Brenda, and I am sure that our family members hold these remembrances close to their hearts.

My sister's death also affected hundreds of people in our community and beyond. She had friends from elementary school, high school, and work, as well as her Newmarket friends and her downtown Toronto friends. So many knew Brenda, and everyone was horror-struck that senseless violence had taken the life of their special friend. Rarely have I met these numbers of kind, caring, and supportive people. It brought great comfort to our family knowing that Brenda had good people in her life and that she was deeply loved.

∞

When I look in the dictionary, "disenfranchised grief" is defined as marginalized, disqualified, or excluded grief. And "complicated grief" means thwarted grief, or grief made more difficult by outside forces.

Some people have wondered if, as a sibling, I ever felt that my grief was disenfranchised. Everyone is different. Although personally I did not feel this way, I recognized that in the early days, there were others close to Brenda who felt their grief was marginalized. Yes, at times friends and acquaintances would neglect to ask how I was coping, perhaps only asking about my parents, but I did not take this personally. And here is how I feel today: as time has moved on, I have realized that I am not in competition with anyone else's grief—this is my journey.

As a sibling deeply affected by my sister's murder, I am hurt beyond any words to describe it. My sister is gone, and my parents never will be the same. A piece of them died that day in 2008, and my children lost a piece of me, their mother, on that day too. Right there and then, this murder impacted three generations. If we do not talk about the "complicated grief" to do with homicide, things will not change. We must break the silence!

Brenda's tragedy shook everyone to the core. Surviving our complicated, many-layered grief was going to be challenging. How do you get through this? What support is there? Through Victim Services, our family slowly opened up to receive help. However, to continue on a healing path, we needed to find a way to help other victims get through this as well. No one should be on this journey alone.

∞

In 2009, partnering with community groups and Victim Services, in honour of Brenda we created "Remember Me: A Homicide Survivor Self-Support Group." This group provides emotional support and helpful information to individuals and families affected by homicide, offering inspiration and hope along with the tools to cope with the tragic loss of a loved one to homicide.

In 2012, our group was awarded the Queen's Diamond Jubilee Award. And in 2013, we were awarded the Attorney General's Victim Services Award of Distinction. I am very proud of our support group. We could not have done it alone. We have had amazing support. And remarkable strength, courage, and determination continue to be shown by our participants year after year.

I miss my sister and she is never far from my thoughts. There are good days and bad days, but I get through them. My family has been forever changed. Naturally, the holidays are not the same without Brenda here, but she is remembered and we are grateful for these memories of her. Brenda would not want us to stay forever sad. She would want us to live and try to do our best every single day—and we do this.

Today my journey through grief continues. With Brenda's murder we have lost pieces of our souls; we mourn our loss and hers. Helping others to cope has been a powerful gift. While giving comfort to others, our self-help group has assisted us too. I am so appreciative that we have been able to do this. Again, I am thankful for the love and support of Brenda's friends, my friends, and our extended family. I am grateful for the love that Brenda and Scott shared. In addition, the support and friendship the Atherton family has given us will never be forgotten. Each bit of warmth, compassion, and kindness has sustained us and helped us to where we are today. Brenda continues to guide us—when I feel like giving up, she sends a sign to help me continue with what I am doing. Thank you, Brenda; truly, I am blessed to have you as my sister.

Now I say to you: please do not give up; continue to reach for what you need. You can make a difference. If I can make it, so can you! If I may, I will close with a poem: a poem that reminds me of my sisters and of how much they mean to me.

Three Sisters

We are three sisters
Three sisters are we
I love each of you,
And I know you love me.

We're not always together,
Life sometimes keeps us apart.
But we're never separated
We're in each other's heart.

Now I know we've had our troubles,
But we always get thru.
The real message is you love me,
And I also love you.
We have had lots of good times
That we'll never forget
Sometimes we worry
And sometimes we fret

But if God ever gave me
Something special you see,
It might have been the blessing of,
Three sisters are we.

By Francis I. Gillespie

Chapter Eight

Robin's Story

Marjorie Suzanne (Suzy) Richardson

Robin Maria Richardson:
October 10, 1986–June 2, 2008

"Reading: A Light in the Darkness"
—Suzy

Robin's Story

There is a complicated tension that exists between our best days and our worst days. Our best days—the ones we look back on as "perfect days"—tend to softly embed themselves in our memories, so that we can go back and visit them whenever the need or want arises. We cling to every detail and try to keep them from fading like a precious photo.

Our worst days—just like our perfect days—also have a way of becoming fixed in our memories. We remember where we were, what we were doing, the sights, the sounds, the smells. And although we would love to be able to release ourselves from the memory of our worst days, we know that, just like our perfect days, we will go back and visit them from time to time.

June 1, 2008 is a day that my mind drifts back to easily. The cloudless sky was ocean-blue, the smell of lilacs hung in the air, and chickadees and cardinals darted in and out among the thick cedar trees that surround our ranch-style bungalow. The warm wind was blowing through the tall hardwoods, and if you closed your eyes it sounded like waves at the beach. Our house is located on a quiet dirt road just outside of town, and we have two-and-a-half acres. We had just built that house the September prior, and with each changing season we were falling more and more in love with it.

The front yard was usually in full sun around 2:00 p.m., so I wasn't surprised when I looked out and saw Robin on the porch, quietly doing a Sudoku. Even at twenty-one, she still looked small in the big Adirondack chair, with her knees drawn up to her chest, making quick work of the puzzle. She had a kooky habit of chewing the side of her tongue when she was concentrating.

As I watched her through the glass of our front door, I chuckled, remembering that when I first noticed this habit of hers she was five and just starting kindergarten. She was learning to tie her shoes and print her last name; now, Robin had just finished her third year of university.

Where had the years gone? It was reassuring to see that even though she had grown, matured, and changed so much since being away at school, some things would never change.

Robin had only been home for about a month, but already she had been extremely busy. She had landed a great summer job with a local accounting firm and was putting in lots of hours. Between her work responsibilities, spending time with her boyfriend in London, and getting caught up with friends at home, Robin was rarely in one spot for any length of time. She had also been dealing with a diagnosed case of iron deficiency anemia and had been to a few hospitals, between home and school, to try to get this issue resolved. The doctors were puzzled and we were concerned but not panicked, based on their reassurances that her condition was nothing serious.

We were all actively trying to get her healthy again. So, in this rare moment of Robin being home and actually sitting and doing nothing, I decided to grab a book and join her on the porch. As I leaned back into the comfort of the chair's deep cushion, I closed my eyes and turned my face upward to soak in as much of the sun as I could. It was like inhaling peace—a feeling that had eluded me for a few months. Momentarily, I was able to exhale and blow away all of the worry that had been stealing so much of my strength and energy.

We didn't say anything to each other while we sat there; we just enjoyed each other's company and let the birds and Mother Nature do all the talking. I remember looking over at Robin on that clear June day, marvelling at what a beautiful young woman she was becoming. Her life held such promise. That realization made me feel proud, but also a bit sad. Since she had arrived back home, I had felt, instinctively, that we should savour the moments we were able to share with Robin because I knew that one day soon she would be leaving us—in the way that all children do—leaving and starting a life of her own. She would go back for one more year at Laurier, then graduate and probably find a job in the city.

I had felt this way on other occasions, but this time it was different—different in a way that I couldn't quite put my finger on.

Later that day, Robin went for an ATV ride with her dad on the trail behind our house, something the two of them had never done before. She wanted her dad to show her how to run his machine and where the trails were, because her boyfriend was coming up to spend the weekend and Robin wanted to take him for a ride.

When I saw the two of them in the driveway, Robin's dad patiently giving instructions, I stood and watched, not wanting the moment to be interrupted. While I was alone in the house I heard a voice: "Run and get the camera!" I was a bit startled, but it seemed like such a good idea that I did not question it. Running to get the camera, I took what would be the last picture ever taken of Robin.

In the evening, Robin organized a trip to the movies with three of her best friends and her younger sister, Kayla. Robin loved life, the way we all should love life. She was always planning get-togethers, trying to make memories and not waste time that could be spent doing something fun or meaningful with friends and family. They went out for the evening and had a wonderful time. In all of its simplicity, it had been a perfect day. Now there exists a great divide between that perfect day, the first of June, and the day that followed.

∞

On June 2, Robin got up to go to work. As I was making her lunch, I asked her how she was feeling. She replied, "Better." Her anemia had been causing shortness of breath, chest pains, and light-headedness, and her hemoglobin was low. I was relieved when she reassured me that she was feeling well enough to go to work.

Later in the day, Robin went out for lunch with some co-workers. She was returning to work when she collapsed on the sidewalk. When her boss called me at the municipal office where I work, I was told that she had fainted. Immediately, I thought this had been due to her low iron.

Robin had been using my car to get to work, so I was without a vehicle. My supervisor volunteered to drive me to the hospital and we left right away.

During the hour-long drive, I called the hospital several times for updates. Each time I was told that she was still unconscious. The nurse on the other end of the phone instructed me, with deliberate calmness, that I should "Just keep coming ... just keep coming."

It is strange what your mind does in an emergency. Fainting normally causes a temporary loss of consciousness; why had I not realized how much time had passed, and that clearly we were dealing with something far more serious? I clung to the word "fainted" and kept thinking that she would wake up. People faint all the time, and it's nothing acute. Robin had been unconscious for at least half an hour, yet in my mind I still was treating it as though she had just fainted, and that it had only been a few minutes.

When we arrived at the hospital, we were taken to an empty trauma room. There wasn't even a bed in it, and there was no sign of Robin. At first, I thought the room was empty because Robin was fine and would come walking out, chastising me for being such a worrywart—something she had done more than once over the last month. Then, after more time had passed, I thought to myself, "She should be here," and I started to sense that the room was empty for a bad reason, not a good one. However, I was trying to remain positive and not overreact.

At one point, someone put some chairs in the room and then the doctor and a nurse came in and asked us to be seated. With a pained look on her face, the doctor said, "I am so sorry; she didn't make it." Initially, I couldn't comprehend what the doctor was telling me—my brain had to make this cataclysmic leap from Robin having fainted to something so dire that I could not grasp it. "She didn't make it ... make what?" I thought to myself. Maybe, in a moment like this, there is no way to comprehend fully, regardless of what words are used. I wonder if I would have understood better if the doctor had said the words "dead" or "died." In the end, the look on the doctor's face said it all; there was no misunderstanding that.

I asked where Robin was, and they guided me to a room next to us. When I first saw her, Robin looked like she was only sleeping. Immediately, I wanted to hold her, but was cautioned that I was to be careful because the coroner had been called and would need to examine everything. I hugged her anyway. As I held Robin, I kept telling her, "I'm sorry, I'm sorry, I'm so sorry" over and over again. Somehow I felt that Robin was able to receive all this love and comfort I was trying to share with her, and also able to hear me speaking to her. I still believe this.

The nurse asked me why I kept saying that I was sorry. I thought this was such an odd question. To me it seemed obvious. As Robin's mother, I should have done a better job of protecting her, a better job of making sure that she received the proper care from the doctors and, most of all, the correct diagnosis.

It felt as if I had completely and utterly failed her.

I am not sure how much time passed before the nurse gently suggested that maybe I should call my family. It simply had not occurred to me; I just wanted to stay with Robin and hold her. Of course, I needed to call my family and felt embarrassed that I had not yet thought to do this. I called my sister-in-law, because I could not bear to tell my husband, Don, over the phone that Robin had died. When he received this traumatic news, I wanted someone to be with him.

There are no words to describe the pain that was shared when I was reunited with my family in the hallway outside of that hospital room. Our old life ended and a new one began. Looking at my face in the mirror of the hospital washroom, I wondered how I could still look the same when something so terrible had happened. The outside of my body seemed curiously oblivious to the devastation and chaos happening on the inside. And this external-internal incongruence continued long after we left the hospital.

People remarked at the funeral how strong we were, how brave we were. It's like a blown lightbulb. You can't tell by the outside if it is working or not; it's only when you shake the lightbulb that you hear all the broken pieces rattling around inside. That's how I felt.

The coroner was called, and we were informed that an autopsy was required. When we were told this, all I could think was "her poor little body." Robin was petite and already she had been through such trauma—it was heartbreaking to think that this was going to take place, although we realized that it was necessary. Our only hope now was that we might be able to find out how and why this had happened.

There was nothing to do next except to go home. As soon as the hospital doors closed behind us and we were in the parking lot, I made another difficult phone call. I had to call Robin's boyfriend. When I finally reached him, I remember saying over and over the same thing I had said to Robin just moments earlier: "I'm so sorry." Not only did I feel responsible for her death, I felt as if I had ruined his life too by not taking better care of her. All of their hopes and dreams together had been stolen away.

The drive home was very quiet, marked with silent sobs, and complete and utter disbelief. When we pulled into the driveway, I looked at the front door knowing that if I walked through that door, all hope that this was some kind of a mistake would be lost

Forty-eight hours later, the coroner called and explained the cause of Robin's death: a pulmonary embolism due to a blood clot. He said we might never know the exact cause. He also advised us to have immediate family members tested for various blood-clotting disorders.

Because the autopsy had taken a few days, we had time to put extra thought into Robin's funeral. On Wednesday evening when the funeral director came to the house, he asked us if there was anything special we wanted to include in the service. Suddenly I remembered a poem Robin had written in her high school Writer's Craft class about our family's bedtime routine when she was a little girl. I had tucked that poem away, thinking maybe I would bring it out when she was a mother and had children of her own. Running to my bedroom, I pulled it out of the old cloth bag that held all of the homemade cards and treasures the girls had given me over the years. The day of the funeral, Robin's poem was read by her creative writing teacher.

"Good Night, I Love You, See You in the Morning"

Three simple phrases said time and time again
Said each night I go to bed since I can't remember when
Each night you say these words to me and each night I hold them close
Of all the words said each day these ones mean the most
They make up for all the hugs we are too afraid to share
They make up for all the tears we pretend are never there
They make up for all the fights that come from time to time
They make up for the anger in your voice and in mine
I know your words will keep me safe and they'll keep my spirit soaring
So for now, good night, I love you, and see you in the morning...

Now her words seem almost prophetic. She has said her good night, she loves us, and she will see us when we are reunited once again. Sometimes I think there is a tendency to put our loved ones on a pedestal, or to wear rose-coloured glasses when looking back on our relationships with them. Her words forced me to acknowledge that although we did have our trials, it was OK. In fact it was normal, and what matters most is the love we shared, not the words we wish we could take back. I cannot go back and change any of the difficult moments, but I can focus on the ones that bring a smile to my face and peace to my heart.

The day after the funeral, when all of our friends and family returned to their daily routines, we awoke to a world we barely recognized. Nothing felt right. Everywhere I went I felt the largeness of her presence and then the void of her absence. I felt as though a part of me was missing—like an amputation.

I drove to the funeral home to collect Robin's belongings, which we had displayed during the visitations: her hockey jersey, her artwork, her guitar. As I stood outside the funeral home and looked at my car across the parking lot, I felt afraid, and did not want to return home. From the moment I had arrived at the hospital on the day Robin died, there had been people there to help us—doctors, nurses, ambulance attendants, and the funeral director—now there was no one telling us where we were to go or what we were supposed to do next. Never having experienced the death of someone so close before Robin's death, I did not know what to expect.

When I was a young girl, my grandfather had died, and it had been shocking. In the days after his funeral, I would close my eyes and try to picture him—not wanting to forget him. But as the days and weeks passed, when I closed my eyes it became harder and harder to picture my grandfather, and sometimes the harder I tried, the more elusive his memory became. It was like chasing a mirage. That was my experience with death. I felt panicked that he was just fading away.

So when I returned home from the funeral home that day, I kept closing my eyes every few minutes to make sure that I could still see Robin in my mind. I was afraid she was going to fade from my memory, and that terrified me. Also, I feared the enormity of her death was going to hit me all at once, and this too alarmed me.

Because of my limited experience with death, I worried that I would be expected to say goodbye to Robin, and I began to wrestle with this notion—it did not feel right. There was so much that I did not understand; perhaps this is why I was drawn so strongly to read about the grieving process. It was an immediate pull.

During that next week we wrote hundreds of thank-you cards—literally. Our small community had collectively wrapped us in their arms and carried us through those dark days. Then, one day, while writing at our kitchen table, I travelled back to a day when Robin was home studying for exams with her business textbooks sprawled all over this very same table. In the background, the BBC's *Planet Earth* series was playing on TV.

Mesmerized, I kept interrupting her study time to say, "Come look at this!" I was so captivated by the beauty, complexity, and absolute magic of nature that I wanted to share it with her. She was patient and polite but really didn't want to be interrupted. That day, watching with the enthusiasm of a child, I felt somehow we were all a part of something much bigger than we know.

After Robin passed, I decided to purchase the DVD series, and ended up watching it whenever I was home alone. It was the only thing that came close to helping me figure out where she was now; I sensed that Robin too was a part of something much bigger than we know. This realization was one of the first things that rang true to me.

∞

Becoming drawn to nature in a way that I never had been before, I began working in the thick bush behind our house and cutting paths through the cedars. When we had bought our land, one of the first things the former owner showed us was an enormous rock situated toward the back of the property. Approximately six feet high and eight feet wide, it ascends mightily from our otherwise flat landscape and is unexpected and awe-inspiring.

This was satisfying, exhausting work, and gave me some comfort ... the solitude, the sounds of the birds, even the snakes were beautiful.

∞

After two weeks of being at home, we went back to work and I felt the need to find other bereaved parents to see how they had survived the death of a child. For some reason, I imagined that other grieving parents held all the answers. A few people had contacted us, and quickly I took them up on their invitations for tea and chats. More often than not, the meetings were helpful, and I am truly grateful to the families who took the time to try to help me. Yet many times I wanted even more of a connection because I felt so alone.

Fearing I would become a burden, I kept my contact with others to a minimum, when really all I craved was to talk to someone who understood how I was feeling—someone who truly "got it." As I think back, I'm pretty sure that they wouldn't have minded; however, self-confidence is a common challenge for a newly bereaved mom.

My brother-in-law mentioned a few times that our first year without Robin would be a very hard year of firsts: our first Christmas without her, birthdays, Mother's Day, Father's Day. He was right. The days and weeks leading up to these important days were filled with dread.

For Robin's birthday, we gathered a bunch of friends and family and drove several ATVs into the bush to release twenty-two white balloons from the highest point on the Bruce Peninsula. It was a beautifully sad day, and I am glad that we did something special to mark this occasion. We wrote messages and attached them to raffia strings; there were even messages from her friends at university.

I put my message in a soup can and burned it. As I watched the grey smoke swirl up and drift away, I felt certain that somehow all of our messages would reach her.

Our first Christmas was worse than I could ever have imagined. The pain and brokenness weighed like a heavy blanket of darkness on us. In December I had tried to shop, but there were constant reminders everywhere that Robin was missing.

Following that first excruciating Christmas, I resolved to shop early, in October, before the stores looked too "Christmas-y"; it has seemed to help. We didn't put up a tree at first, but then I thought that our house was already sad enough. It would seem even sadder if the spot for the tree was empty.

Christmas morning, I wished that I could take some of Don and Kayla's pain away, but I couldn't. I was completely helpless. Their pain was unreachable.

We live in a very small town, and at the time of Robin's passing, there were precious few bereavement supports in our community; therefore, reading books written by other bereaved parents became my lifeline. In the middle of the night, when the pain of Robin's death would not let me sleep, I would pick up a book and be comforted by the words of other parents who had travelled ahead of me on this grief journey. It was like having a conversation with all of these people, and yet I didn't feel as if I was intruding on their privacy. They answered many of the painful questions burning within me, without me having to garner the courage to ask. Gripped by their stories, I often found myself, Don, and Kayla in the pages of these books.

While it's true that for some bereaved people, support groups and healthcare professionals play essential roles in the healing process, I believe that reading fiction, non-fiction, and poetry is undervalued and underestimated as a healing aid. Books of all genres can be practical and economical resource companions for those struggling with the loss of a loved one.

Quite often, when a family suffers the loss of a child, the first six months can be very lonely. Some grief support groups require participants to wait at least six months before they can join. For those seeking professional counselling, it is not uncommon to be placed on a waiting list before getting a first appointment. So it is at this juncture that I think reading can be of the greatest importance—the power of the written word shining bright in some very dark places.

One of the first books I had an opportunity to read was called *Journaling a Pathway Through Grief* (by Wendy Dean); I accessed it through our lovely local library. When I finished reading it, I felt a tremendous sense of awe that the author had found the strength to write about her daughter's death, and said to myself, "Wow, I could never do that, but I am glad that somebody else did." I learned so much from her private admissions and those of her husband and son.

There were so many aspects of Robin's death I wrestled with; when I read that Wendy had struggled with some of these same things, I didn't feel so alone. This would prove to be the case with many of the stories I would go on to read. Upon learning that some parents found going back to work helpful, I felt a great relief. Returning to work after only two weeks, I had experienced feelings of guilt. But with a new house and a new mortgage, I had also begun to worry about our finances. For me, it was the right thing to do and I do not judge the choices of others.

As well, I felt less guilty when I read that good friends and a glass of wine helped others process their grief (while paying attention to the cautions of developing too much of an appetite for alcohol and/or other vices—which can sometimes be a concern with the vulnerabilities of loss).

I struggled with the fact that Kayla, Don, and I did not have long discussions about our loss of Robin; I thought I was failing them by not being able to talk freely. Soon I discovered that this is not uncommon. Over time I have come to appreciate and admire how we have respected each other's pain. As a family, we have shared it in our own way. There is no right or wrong way to grieve. What helps one person may hinder another.

∞

One day, shortly after Robin passed, I happened to stop in to a Salvation Army thrift store and found an entire collection of some of the most noteworthy books on grief. Purchasing them all for approximately ten dollars, I couldn't believe my good fortune. I felt a tremendous gratitude toward the generous stranger who had made such a wonderful donation, and still do to this day. I read and re-read those books several times: Rabbi Kushner's *When Bad Things Happen to Good People*; C.S. Lewis's *A Grief Observed*; Viktor Frankl's *Man's Search For Meaning*; Hope Edelman's *Motherless Daughters*, and many, many more. All of these books spoke to my crushed and diminished spirit.

Since then I have passed on these treasures, even though I hated to part with them. Now I pick up books whenever I can and give them to people who are grieving, or to groups and agencies supporting the bereaved.

I have found that we are individual in the ways in which we learn to live with our losses. My story is just that—mine—and only I know what has helped me. I have met many people who have never felt the need to pick up a book and then there are others who have mini-libraries like I do. We are different and this is okay. Sometimes I wish I could be more like Don and Kayla, but I am me, so I just keep following my own heart.

∞

In the days and weeks after Robin's death, although I went to church and clung to my faith, a very intense internal struggle began to emerge. As it turned out, my faith in God could not hold the weight of my loss and slowly began to crack under the stress of my grief until it completely crumbled. Praying felt like begging that never worked. The whole notion of heaven and hell, and who goes where, felt very complicated to me. Coming to the conclusion that something so eternally important should not be this confusing, I had to let it go. Although this was terrifying at first, it was a necessary process that helped restore some peace back into my life. While I do my very best to try to make some sense out of life's most difficult questions, I figure God's not going anywhere.

My questioning has forced me to dig deeper to try to find out what I truly believe. My faith is like a chalkboard that has been wiped clean. It is blank now but I don't think it will always be this way. When the words are rewritten, they will be more permanent and not so easily wiped away.

Something else I have struggled with is the fact that Robin died a preventable death. She died of a pulmonary embolism. What she needed was a CT scan. She never got one. In the month that she had been home from school, we had been seen by several different doctors, between trips to the ER and appointments with the doctors who were treating her anemia. Each time we were told that there was nothing serious going on, or that there was no explanation for what was going on. And each time we were sent home. For anyone who has lost a loved one to a preventable/treatable death, you know how disturbing this is.

When I review the details, I know exactly the point at which I think I could have/should have saved Robin's life.

One day I shared my regrets and my feelings of guilt with parents who were also suffering with the deaths of their children. I said to them, "There was one day when we were driving home from the hospital and Robin still wasn't feeling well. Worrying that something more serious was going on, I almost took her to another ER—but I didn't. If I had trusted my instincts, Robin would still be here." These parents looked me straight in the eye and said, with a deeper understanding than most, "You don't know that for sure."

How could they say this when I felt so certain? I could tell that after years of living with this kind of pain, they had come to the realization that no amount of speculating would bring me any closer to the truth—or closer to truly knowing how different choices would have affected Robin's outcome. Inexplicably, on that particular day I finally grasped the wisdom in their words.

Perhaps going to a different hospital would have saved Robin. Or maybe, yet again, we would have been sent home and nothing would have changed. Or this might have given her one more chance for life. But never, ever, will I know for sure. Now I try not to torture myself by constantly going back over it.

Through our sorrow, I like to think that we have done something worthwhile—something to ensure that other families might be spared the same pain. The coroner's office conducted an investigation—not an inquest—and looked at all the facts concerning Robin's death. We petitioned them on a regular basis to ensure they had all of the facts and to make sure that her case did not get buried under a stack of papers, lest she become just another case number.

∞

After almost two years, we were given the Coroner's Investigation Statement. There were several errors in the report, which I spotted right away, but the Investigation Statement read, "There were concerns raised by Robin's mother around her death; specifically, whether this could have been prevented or diagnosed sooner." It went on to say that "both hospitals involved would be asked to perform a case review to develop recommendations to prevent deaths, in similar circumstances, in the future." Reading all of these details about what had happened in the ER the day Robin died was traumatic for us. It was like reliving that terrible day all over again. But it helped to know steps would be taken to prevent future deaths.

Trying to remember that all of the doctors and nurses who attended to Robin tried to do their best, I have strived to keep any bitterness toward the hospitals from overtaking my life. No one intentionally meant to miss her diagnosis. I wouldn't want to be a doctor and am grateful for the hospital in our community. Also, I do believe something has been gleaned from our situation that will help someone else down the road.

When I spoke to a doctor about Robin's case report, I remember he seemed very surprised that two hospitals were being asked to do a case review. In all of his years as a physician, he had never seen this happen. He made it seem as if we had achieved some kind of great feat. I did not feel that way at all. I told him that at the very least we owed it to Robin to make sure her case was reviewed, and that she deserved so much more.

Much of the first two years after Robin's passing was consumed faxing and emailing the coroner's office. It was a long, difficult process and even though it did nothing to change our circumstances, I feel we accomplished something very worthwhile.

∞

Having had a few years now to look back on our loss, the most reassuring thought I have is that grieving has never been about saying goodbye to Robin. Rather, it has been about learning how to carry her with us as we move through our own lives. Even if I do not know for certain what lies beyond this life, I do not feel that Robin has ceased to exist. Sometimes I feel her very strongly: when I listen to her music, when I smell her perfume, see her friends, look at old pictures, and especially while looking at Kayla. When it hurts the most, that's when I feel her the most. Never do I want this to change. I have had dreams where I have seen Robin, and they have felt so real that I wish I could close my eyes each night and see her. But this does not happen—and I cannot conjure them up either. The dreams and the feelings of her presence are fleeting gifts.

What helps me the most, I find, is when I am actively doing something I believe will honour her life. Robin received a few blood transfusions during her short illness, and they made her feel better. I remember feeling tremendous gratitude toward the people who donate blood. The first time I donated was after Robin's death, and it was a meaningful experience. There are very few things we can do in this life that actually help improve another's life and make a tangible difference; this simple but oh-so-important gift is one of them. I believe that organ donation is another truly significant way we can give the gift of life and have signed my organ donor card.

Two awards created in Robin's memory are very near and dear to our hearts. One is an endowment set up at Sir Wilfrid Laurier University by Robin's employer, BDO Dunwoody Chartered Accountants, in conjunction with Don and me. The other is a creative writing award at Robin's high school, established by Don, my family, and me. Robin's life continues to impact others and this means so much to us.

I wear a ring that Robin bought while on a high school trip to Italy, France, and Spain, and a silver emblem of a bird on a chain given to me by a friend. These talismans remind me that she is with me always.

∞

This journey has taught me to savour special moments with the people who are still in my life. I remember sitting with my dad at my kitchen table the first Thanksgiving after Robin had passed. Even though I did not feel like celebrating and did not feel particularly thankful, I did have the sense he would not always be with me, and felt gratitude that we were able to be with each other making memories that day. Dad died a few years later, and I cherish all of the times we spent together before he left this world.

I am blessed to have a very loving, understanding, and strong husband, and I admire the many ways that he carries Robin in his heart. It is his steadiness that keeps me going. If I get lost in my sadness, it's usually Don who shows me the way out of it. On some of our hardest days I often look at him and think, "If he can do it, I can do it too." Our daughter, Kayla, is simply the greatest joy in our lives. She continues to bloom into the most beautiful person. She has an old soul for someone so young. Kayla will be married soon, and her fiancé is a welcome addition to our family—he has a very kind heart. Robin was in love with a wonderful young man when she passed; he keeps in touch with us, and we share a bond that will never be broken.

Still, I worry from time to time that Robin's presence will fade. I quiet those fears by reminding myself that she is very much a part of my life, even if I can't see her or touch her. If you drop a stone into deep water, it creates a cloud of sand when it hits the bottom. But if you wait and let the sand settle, then you can see the stone on the bottom. You might not be able to reach it, but you know it's there. That's what my life is like now. If I become anxious about Robin and start churning up the water, I lose sight of her. But eventually my heart and my mind become calm, and when the turbidity settles back down I can see her clearly again. She is beyond my physical reach, but not beyond the reach of my heart.

∞

I have come across many symbols and signs that people gravitate to when they are trying to understand, explain, or relate to their grief: butterflies, dragonflies, feathers, pennies, dimes; they all seem to hold a deep meaning and a connection to loved ones. But a symbol that I cherish, and one that symbolizes our survival, is grass. Not what you were expecting, I am sure, but let me explain.

Grass is an incredibly amazing and resilient plant. It covers more of Earth's land and feeds more wildlife than any other plant. It is vitally important to this planet. It can also survive in the most severe conditions. When the stress of a drought occurs, the roots go down deep, making the grass stronger. When naturally occurring wildfires ignite grasslands, everything in their path is wiped out. Lush plains can be reduced to smoldering charred soil in minutes. The amazing thing about this phenomenon is that somehow, after a fire, new life emerges from the ashes. With the tiniest amounts of rain, in the most uninhabitable conditions, tiny shoots will begin to grow because grass, as it turns out, is almost indestructible; it grows from deep down at the very base of its stems.

After June 2, 2008, my life was like dry grassland and Robin's death sparked a fire that consumed everything I had put any faith in. When the smoke finally settled, I was left with a dead and barren landscape where my happy life had been. But somewhere, deep within, there was a small stem of hope that survived, and very slowly, with a great deal of effort, new life began to emerge.

It has taken me a long time to be able to put these words down on paper, and I still do not understand why all of this happened to us. But I understand not all questions have answers. At peace with knowing that our love for Robin will never end, I am sustained by the fact that the world is a beautiful, complex, mysterious, and wondrous place, which makes it difficult to believe we are all here by accident. Remember the camera incident? I don't have an explanation for that either, but I am glad it happened.

When I reflect on our terrible loss, with all of its incredible pain and heartache, I grieve for all that has been taken from us. Yet I never cease to be amazed by love, life, and the human spirit, and how they—like the simple miracle of green grass—are almost indestructible.

Afterword

"We don't receive wisdom; we must discover it for ourselves, after a journey that no one can take for us, or spare us." —Marcel Proust

Life Came to a Standstill is the book I searched for at the beginning of my grief journey—a book offering validation and hope in the midst of deep sorrow. With the violence of an unexpected death, those left behind to mourn may experience levels of trauma that can cause them to feel they are going mad. We assure you that you are not crazy. You are in grief. It is essential to just *breathe*.

By not giving up, the writers of these stories have found ways to continue with their lives—lives that have changed forever. Each of us is learning, one day at a time, to move forward with hope. We understand that what honours our children best is for us to make positive differences in our own lives, as well as in the lives of others.

Please know that we, the seven bereaved mothers and one bereaved sister who share our stories in *Life Came to a Standstill*, do not do so as professionals or as therapists, regardless of the further education that some of our writers have accomplished. These narratives are derived from personal experiences with bereavement. During these journeys, although we have become experts in our own grief, we do not profess that what has helped us is the only path for others. Rather, we recommend that you reach out for professional guidance and follow your heart to find the coping tools that speak to you.

In the subsequent pages, please take comfort from the selected wise counsel of the following three educators, well respected in their chosen fields of work and study.

First, *The Myth of Closure*, by Ashley Davis Bush LISCW, author and therapist: Ashley's insightful article will lend you validation while answering some of the burning questions about your grief journey. Next, *We Choose to Read: Bibliotherapy and Memories of Loss and Grief*, by Dr. Hoi F. Cheu, Associate Professor, Laurentian University, past president of the Association for Bibliotherapy and Applied Literature. Dr. Cheu's article illuminates the immeasurable therapeutic value of reading.

While my passion for books has been life-long, until recently I did not recognize the word bibliotherapy. Still, there have been times when a specific book, or a special text, has given me just enough strength to take the next step. Perhaps it will shine a warm light of understanding on you, as it has on me.

Last but not least, lean into the life-affirming wisdom of *Helping Yourself Heal After Someone Loved Dies*, by Dr. Alan Wolfelt, a well-respected author and educator in the crucial areas of loss and healing.

∞

In closing, I will share an encouraging metaphor with you. One evening, while I facilitated a child-loss session, Bruce, a bereaved dad, revealed to our group that each caring word and compassionate gesture has added an important brick to the construction of his bridge: a coping bridge to span the chasm of his deep grief.

Afterword

We wish you faith, endurance, and hope in the construction of your healing/coping bridge. If you find yourself in doubt or in trouble, please ask for help. Above all else, do not give up. Thank you for choosing to read.

"Love is space and time measured by the heart." —*Marcel Proust*

— Gwendolyn Broadmore

Addendum

The Myth of Closure

Ashley Davis Bush
LISCW, author of *Transcending Loss* as well as *Hope and Healing for Transcending Loss* (www.ashleydavisbush.com)

- When faced with grief we often ask, "When will I begin to feel better? When will I return to normal? When will I achieve some closure?" The idea of closure in our culture is one of tidy endings, a sense of completion. The reason we long for closure, of course, is because we would like to be rid of this pain. We would like to shut out the sad, confused, desperate, angry feelings from our lives, putting all of this pain behind us so that we can feel joy again.

- For some of us, we expect "closure" to happen after the funeral or memorial service or after a loved one's room has been cleared out. For others, we look for closure after a personal ritual or after the first anniversary comes and goes. "Surely, then we will have closure," we think. We pray.

- But what an odd concept really, closure … as if we could turn the lock and throw away the key, as if we could truly close the door on our emotions and our love for someone lost. The truth, of course, is far more complex. The "closure" that we all strive for loses its relevancy in the realms of loss and love.

195

- Closure may work well in the world of practical matters—
  with business deals and real estate transactions. But closure
  does not apply to the human heart, not in a pure sense. It
  isn't possible to permanently close the door on the past as if
  it didn't exist. And why would we want to anyway … really?
  If we were so thoroughly detached from our loss, we would
  not only close the door on the pain, we would also sever the
  connection to our loved one.
- In losing someone dear to us, it's important to remember
  that the relationship itself is not over. Death cannot take
  away the love that weaves its way through every fibre of our
  being. Love will always triumph over death in this regard.
  We want to hold our cherished memories close to our
  heart, recognizing that our love is an essential part of us. In
  fact, we want to open the door, not close it, onto the reality
  of living with loss.
- Perhaps it is better to drop the idea of closure and think
  instead in terms of healing and growth. We can process our
  pain and move to deeper and deeper levels of healing; we
  can find ways to move on while holding our relationship
  with our loved one forever in our hearts; we can channel
  our pain into meaningful activities to honour our loved
  ones; we can even learn to smile again, laugh again, breathe
  again, and love again.
- Our loss becomes love transformed, transformed from that
  which relies on physical presence to something more pure.
  So let us not strive for closure. When we do that, we unwittingly close the door on all the love that we shared. And,
  truly, that would be a loss too terrible to bear.

—Ashley Davis Bush

We Choose to Read: Bibliotherapy and Memories of Loss and Grief

Dr. Hoi F. Cheu

Associate professor, Department of English, Laurentian University and winner of the 2011 Teaching Excellency Award; Specializing in arts-based health research and documentary filmmaking, Dr. Cheu teaches literary theory, modernist literature, and film production. He has been trained in family therapy and is past president of the Association for Bibliotherapy and Applied Literature.

Let me begin with a quote from Chapter Three of *Life Came to a Standstill*: within *Adrian's Story*, Helen Jay reflects:

> Reading what and when I could—curling up with a book in my own personal refuge—though not for everyone, for me was healing. While I absorbed the experiences of others, I was free to weep, laugh, reject, or accept the written words. No one was watching. No one could correct or shame me. Reading was a safe, cerebral space where I could take my time adjusting to and mapping the alien landscape of grief in complete silence and privacy.
>
> Gaining knowledge about grief normalized it and helped alleviate some of the loneliness associated with the many challenging days, weeks, and months. It validated the intense emotions bombarding me, assuring me that I was not out of my mind as I struggled through a world resembling fogged lunacy. Reading helped promote thought; it helped clarify who and where I was.

It seems to me that without perhaps identifying it, Helen was choosing the solace and healing comfort of bibliotherapy. The purpose of storytelling is more than communication. We build our identities, our sense of purpose, our thinking, and our emotional richness through stories. Because we are a symbolic species, language is a tool of our consciousness. Consequently, stories constitute our identity formation. Remembering, telling, or even making up stories is a human way of organizing, modelling, and exploring the possibilities of life.

In this sense, bibliotherapy is drawing on the most evolved human resource for healing and coping. This human resource is as ancient as languages: i.e., we have been telling stories for millennia—to entertain, to communicate emotions, to pass down wisdom, and to share lives. The advantages of reading literature are specific: the act of reading can be private, and the stories that one can read are not from one's own life. In stories, we do not need to deal with our own lives directly, thus transferring difficult emotions to the fictional space.

Sharing other people's stories helps us to ease the feeling of being alone. Yet because the stories are not the readers' own, the readers can respond, feed back and feed forward more easily. The readers can transfer negative feelings like sadness and anger to the "people" constructed in their minds through the words. Difficult life situations can be sorted out, tried out, and cried out in the minds of the readers.

We are all human. Sooner or later, we all have loved ones who will leave us. We all have to confront our own mortality. We need to explore the feelings and the thoughts of people who have struggled with their own loss and grief. Instead of feeling "woe is me," we find bravery in others. We do not need to wait until we have to deal with our own difficulties in order to read about them. Reading can be preventive medicine. It is true that death, or serious loss of any kind, requires us to look back, but we can also look ahead with other people's stories. We go back and forth in time with stories.

For a moment, let us turn to Dr. Sigmund Freud (1856–1939), the founder/father of psychoanalysis. Toward the later part of his career, through clinical observation and life experience, Freud began to realize that the pleasure principle (a psychoanalytic term coined by Dr. Freud), which identified the human drive to seek pleasure and to avoid pain, had great limitations in explaining how people cope with physical and emotional traumas. In *Beyond the Pleasure Principle* (1920), he attempted to theorize the human need to relive pain and suffering. Although it provided great insights, the essay was never as popular as his concept of the Oedipus complex, partly because (in my view) the topic does not inspire the hedonist modern culture founded on the pleasure principle.

Our culture sometimes delivers surprises, however. Pixar Studio's 2015 release, *Inside Out* (Pete Docter and Ronnie del Carmen), makes an implicit critique of hedonism and the pleasure principle. The film tells the story of an eleven-year-old girl named Riley. She is a happy child. Inside her mind are "little people"—Joy, Sadness, Anger, Fear, and Disgust—representing various emotional functions of the brain. Of course, Joy dominates. But as the girl grows towards puberty, her family moves to San Francisco—away from her Midwestern town, where she played hockey and enjoyed her friends. She is unhappy in her new home, and yet her family needs her to act happy (or at least she perceives that this is the case).

To maintain her control so that Riley can stay happy, Joy draws a circle on the floor and tells Sadness to stand inside the circle because the happy memories turn blue when she touches them. The attempt to suppress Sadness dismantles Riley's ability to cope and eventually leads to her mental breakdown. It is a difficult journey (and action-packed, of course) for Joy to discover the important role of Sadness in Riley's recovery.

Obviously, the story is an analogy of our psychological balance. On a socio-political level, moreover, it offers a critique of our culture's tendencies to celebrate happy consumers, and "cast out" serious writers and intellectual critics. Generally, it is difficult for us to tell sad stories and share experiences of loss and grief. We feel guilty for making others sad. We worry about exposing the dark corners of our inner worlds. Describing emotional pain sometimes feels worse than standing naked in public. So many people draw a circle to keep Sadness from touching their memories. It takes a healing journey and tremendous courage to "tell."

∞

What is the importance of telling or reading sorrowful stories? Although its observations are important and the thinking deep, Freud's *Beyond the Pleasure Principle* does not explain the human interest in reliving and exploring painful experiences by acting out, speaking out, or reading stories about other people confronting loss and grief. Freud supposes that the compulsion to re-enact pain and grief is the result of a "death drive" (an instinct to return to an earlier inorganic state). Although he struggles with this strange phenomenon, he believes that the compulsion to repeat unpleasant habits, dreams, and stories are the symbolic manifestation of this death drive, which to Freud appears primitive and irrational.

With the knowledge of almost a century of research and practice in psychotherapy behind it, however, *Inside Out* may portray a different mental mechanism at work in the compulsion to repeat. I will call it a "survival drive." It is a highly evolved brain function.

Just like Freud's grandson playing the fort/da game to cope with the "loss" of his mother (refer to *Beyond the Pleasure Principle*, Freud 1920), we use the symbolic realm of our mind to deal with difficult moments in our lives.

Bibliotherapy assumes this survival drive: people read because they are coping. The term refers to the use of reading as a means for healing. Although it is only getting better known recently in North America, bibliotherapy has a long history. There is no exact time of its beginning.

C. Perryman has surveyed the use of the hospital library for therapeutic and counselling purposes, and his work covers the years from 1790 to 1950. The field under the name "Bibliotherapy" certainly began in the nineteenth century. On a very basic level, Bibliotherapy is about using books—particularly literature—for mental or even physical health. It can simply be giving prescriptions of stories for people to deal with certain life issues, just like using medicine for relieving symptoms and curing diseases.

It is not as simple as telling people to read a happy story when they are sad. Indeed, we often read sad stories to confront our sadness, to share our misery, in order to manage emotional pain. Stories can provide information, aid understanding, nurture empathy, reframe thinking, provoke emotional response, and share dangerous thoughts in the safe world of storytelling and reading.

Storytelling is not an art; instead, every art form, each in its own way, tells stories. Storytelling is a survival strategy. Medical anthropologist Terrance Deacon refers to human beings as "the symbolic species," meaning that the human brain co-evolves with the development of language. Contemporary knowledge in neuroplasticity has also brought new insights into the understanding of bibliotherapy. In *The Brain That Changes Itself*, Norman Doidge describes our brain as "the Culturally Modified Brain." He elaborates:

Neuroplastic research has shown us that every
sustained activity ever mapped—including physical activities, sensory activities, learning, thinking, and imagining —changes the brain as well
as the mind. Cultural ideas and activities are no
exception. Our brains are modified by the cultural activities we do—be they reading, studying
music, or learning new languages. We all have
what might be called a culturally modified brain,
and as cultures evolve, they continually lead to
new changes in the brain … So a neuroplasti-
cally informed view of culture and the brain
implies a two-way street: the brain and genetics
produce culture, but culture also shapes the brain.
Sometimes these changes can be dramatic. (288)

Of Doidge's three examples of "cultural activities," reading
and learning new languages are obviously language-based, and
the third, bearing in mind that Henry Wadsworth Longfellow
describes music as the universal language of humankind, is argu-
ably about language as well. The arts of language, music, and literature enhance the brain of the symbolic species. In other words,
we now have the scientific knowledge to demonstrate that cultural
activities can change brain structures.

The field of literature can now work with scientists to inves-
tigate a biological approach to storytelling: literature or complex
storytelling in any art form (be it movies, music, theatre, or even
painting) is natural and beneficial to "the symbolic species." After
Deacon, therefore, Joseph Gold (Bibliotherapist and professor of
literature) suggests that we may as well describe humans as "the
story species." Our brains are built for stories and stories can
change our brains.

Addendum

Why is "story" pivotal to the evolution of the brain in such a way that, according to Deacon, most of the higher brain functions are founded on its symbolic activities? According to the basic principle of evolution, the answer has to be that language and storytelling work in favour of the species' survival. But how is it so? To illustrate the role of language, I often invite my students of rhetoric to look around the classroom and find one thing that they can make all by themselves from scratch. Whether as simple as a piece of paper or as complicated as a cell phone, no one single individual in any of my classes has ever found one thing that he or she can make from scratch. The human society, as a complex system, produces the goods. One can image what happens if we take language out of the system: workers not called, schedules not maintained, knowledge not transferred, ideas not communicated, and problems not solved. For a social animal, communication is vital to survival.

Not surprisingly, the surviving text of Aristotle's *Poetics* pays much attention to tragedy. Tragedy has healing powers. People need it. They need, as Aristotle puts it, "catharsis" to purge their negative emotions. Sometimes, people read sad stories (or watch sad movies) not because they are driven by a death instinct, but because it is a survival technique. In the end of *Inside Out*, Joy and Sadness join hands. When they touch the memories, mono-colour turns into a rainbow.

In stories, we are not alone: in stories, we join the whole human species in history; we pass on our wisdom to generations to come. We learn through dark emotions. It is a matter of survival. But the paradox is that darkness overwhelms. Stories can lighten the darkness by making rainbows. Such is the power and relevance of the stories in *Life Came to a Standstill*. We thank the writers for sharing their experiences, and for their talent of storytelling, which gives us the gift of hope.

—Hoi F. Cheu

Works Cited:

Deacon, T. 1997. *The Symbolic Species*. New York: W. W. Norton & Company.

Doidge, N. 2007. *The Brain That Changes Itself.* New York: Viking.

Freud, S. 1920. *Beyond the Pleasure Principle*. In *The Standard Edition of the Complete Psychological Works of Sigmund Freud, Volume XVIII.* Translated by James Strachey, 1955. Toronto: The Hogarth Press.

Gold, J. 2003. *The Story Species: Our Life-Literature Connection.* Markham: Fitzhenry & Whiteside.

Perryman, C. 2006. "Medicus Deus: A review of factors affecting hospital library services to patients between the years 1790–1950." *Journal of the Medical Library Association, 94* (3), 263–270.

Helping Yourself Heal When Someone Loved Dies

Dr. Alan Wolfelt
Respected author and educator on the topic of healing in grief, serves as the Director of the Center for Loss and Life Transitions in Fort Collins, Colorado, U.S.A. (www.centerforloss.com)

Someone you love has died. You are now faced with the difficult, but important, need to mourn. Mourning is the open expression of your thoughts and feelings regarding the death and the person who has died. It is an essential part of healing. You are beginning a journey that is often frightening, painful, overwhelming, and sometimes lonely. This article provides practical suggestions to help you move toward healing in your personal grief experience.

- Realize your grief is unique;

Your grief is unique. No one will grieve in exactly the same way. Your experience will be influenced by a variety of factors: the relationship you had with the person who died, the circumstances surrounding the death, your emotional support system, and your cultural and religious background.

As a result of these factors, you will grieve in your own special way. Don't try to compare your experience with that of other people or to adopt assumptions about just how long your grief should last. Consider taking a "one-day-at-a-time" approach that allows you to grieve at your own pace.

- Talk about your grief;

Express your grief openly. By sharing your grief outside yourself, healing occurs. Ignoring grief won't make it go away; talking about it often makes you feel better. Allow yourself to speak from your heart, not just your head. Doing so doesn't mean you are losing control or going "crazy." It is a normal part of your grief journey.

Find caring friends and relatives who will listen without judging. Seek out those persons who will "walk with" not "in front of" or "behind" you in your journey through grief. Avoid persons who are critical or who try to steal your grief from you. They may tell you, "Keep your chin up," or "Carry on," or "Be happy." While these comments may be well-intended, you do not have to accept them. You have a right to express your grief; no one has the right to take it away.

- Expect to feel a multitude of emotions;

Experiencing loss affects your head, heart, and spirit. So you may experience a variety of emotions as a part of your grief work. Confusion, disorganization, fear, guilt, or relief, are just a few of the explosive emotions you may feel. Sometimes these emotions will follow each other within a short period of time, or they may occur simultaneously.

As strange as some of these emotions may seem, they are normal and healthy. Allow yourself to learn from these feelings. And don't be surprised if out of nowhere you suddenly experience surges of grief, even at the most unexpected times. These grief attacks can be frightening and leave you feeling overwhelmed. They are, however, a natural response to the death of someone loved. Find someone who understands your feelings and will allow you to talk about them.

- Allow for numbness;

Feeling dazed or numb when someone dies is often part of the early grief experience. This numbness serves a valuable purpose; it gives your emotions time to catch up with what your mind has told you. This feeling helps create insulation from the reality of the death until you are more able to tolerate what you don't want to believe.

- Be tolerant of your physical and emotional limits;

Your feelings of loss and sadness will probably leave you fatigued. Your ability to think clearly and make decisions may be impaired. And your low energy level may naturally slow you down. Respect what your body and mind are telling you. Nurture yourself. Get daily rest. Eat balanced meals. Lighten your schedule as much as possible. Caring for yourself doesn't mean feeling sorry for yourself; it means you are using survival skills.

- Develop a support system;

Reaching out to others and accepting support is often difficult, particularly when you hurt so much. But the most compassionate self-action you can do at this difficult time is to find a support system of caring friends and relatives who will provide the understanding you need. Find those people who encourage you to be yourself and acknowledge your feelings—both happy and sad.

• Make use of ritual;
The funeral ritual does more than acknowledge the death of someone loved. It helps provide you with the support of caring people. Most important, the funeral is a way for you to express your grief outside yourself. If you eliminate this ritual, you often set yourself up to repress your feelings, and you can cheat everyone who cares of the chance to pay tribute to someone who was, and always will be, loved.

• Embrace your spirituality;
If faith is a part of your life, express it in ways that seem appropriate to you. Allow yourself to be around people who understand and support your religious beliefs. If you are angry at God because of the death of someone you loved, realize this feeling as a normal part of your grief work. Find someone to talk with who won't be critical of your feelings of hurt and abandonment. You may hear someone say, "With faith, you don't need to grieve." Don't believe it. Having your personal faith does not insulate you from needing to talk out and explore your thoughts and feelings. To deny your grief is to invite problems that build up inside you. Express your faith, but express your grief as well.

• Allow a search for meaning;
You may find yourself asking, "Why did he die?"; "Why this way?"; "Why now?" This search for meaning is often another part of the healing process. Some questions have answers. Some do not. Actually, the healing occurs in the opportunity to pose the questions, not necessarily in answering them. Find a supportive friend who will listen responsively as you search for meaning.

- Treasure your memories;

Memories are one of the best legacies that exist after someone loved dies. Treasure them. Share them with your family and friends. Recognize that your memories may make you laugh or cry. In either case, they are a lasting part of the relationship that you had with a very special person in your life.

- Move toward your grief and heal;

The capacity to love requires the necessity to grieve when someone loved dies. You cannot heal unless you openly express your grief. Denying your grief will only make it become more confusing and overwhelming. Embrace your grief and heal.

Reconciling your grief will not happen quickly. Remember grief is a process, not an event. Be patient and tolerant with yourself. Never forget that the death of someone loved changes your life forever. It's not that you won't be happy again. It's simply that you will never be exactly the same as you were before the death. The experience of grief is powerful. So, too, is your ability to help yourself heal. In doing the work of grieving, you are moving toward a renewed sense of meaning and purpose in your life.

—Dr. Alan Wolfelt

Acknowledgements and Credits

We are thankful to our eight families and to our friends for their faith in us, and apologize that within our narratives there are many whom we failed to mention by name. You know who you are, and your ongoing support has been essential.

Erwin, your patience throughout these many years of planning, writing, and compiling has meant the world to me. Thank you, my love, for your endurance.

My sincere gratitude to my fellow writers: Carol Reid-LeClair, Helen Jay, Janet Rice, Beverley Ogus, Kathleen Stevens, Susan Massey, and Marjorie Suzanne (Suzy) Richardson. I admire your courage in travelling back to the darkness of the early days. I am indebted to your willingness to share your grief journeys in order to offer validation to others. Without your candour and trust, this book could not have been born.

Photo credits, and my deep appreciation, for the cover and the author's photo, go to photographer Roger LeBuffe of Stouffville, Ontario.

Thanks to Catherine Graham for the permission to reprint her thought-provoking poems: "Window Washer Sings at the Terminal," and "The Ritual," from *The Red Element* (Insomniac Press 2008).

Our warm acknowledgements: to Kelly Foxton for her heart-lifting poems, "Six Healing Prayers," and to Francis I. Gillespie for her poignant rhyme, "Three Sisters."

Gratitude to Dr. Alan Wolfelt for permission to reprint his work, *Helping Yourself Heal When Someone Loved Dies*; to Ashley Davis Bush, LICSW, for *The Myth of Closure*; and to Hoi F. Cheu (PhD), for *We Choose to Read: Bibliotherapy and Memories of Loss and Grief*, as well as for Dr. Cheu's uplifting quote on our front cover.

Not to forget our early readers: Patricia, Harold, Phyllis, Coralie, Donna, Lynn, Christel, Perry, Leonore, Claire, Maureen, and Patti; without your help we would have been lost.

We give special kudos to Debbie Gilbert for her invaluable patient editing assistance in the early days of *Life Came to a Standstill*. And a separate mention to the editor at FriesenPress for her remarkable abilities and unfailing eye for detail. In fact, all of the helpmates at FriesenPress have consistently and tirelessly imparted knowledge and support, most especially Publishing Specialist, Sarah Mitchell—thank you.

And our deep thankfulness regarding "Praise for *Life Came to a Standstill*" to:

- Dr. Stephen Fleming, PhD, C, Psych., Emeritus Professor and Senior Scholar, Department of Psychology, Faculty of Health, York University, Toronto, Ontario.
- Christine Goguen, Services Coordinator, Bereaved Families of Ontario-York Region.
- Christine Evain, Assistant Professor, Ecole Centrale de Nantes, France.

About the Writers

- **Gwendolyn Broadmore** lives in Ontario with her husband and their opinionated parrot, Blue. The sudden, violent death of her son, Liam, as well as the stories of the countless bereaved parents, who have shared their pain with her, inspired this book. In the early days of her grief, Gwen found that reading the stories of others carried and consoled her. She hopes that *Life Came to a Standstill* will likewise provide validation and encouragement to those who struggle with the deep anguish of sorrow and the loneliness of loss. Gwen's first publication, *Grief and the Courts*, a not-for-profit booklet resource for surviving victims of violent crime, is available online.

- **Carol Reid-LeClair** is the mother of two children: daughter Christine and son Alan, who died tragically in December, 2005. In a search for answers to her sudden, mind-numbing grief, Carol read everything she could find on surviving the death of a child. During her painful journey, Carol met Gwendolyn Broadmore at a bereavement support group. When asked if she would contribute to *Life Came to a Standstill*, Carol instantly said, "yes." She strongly believes that this book's true accounts of traumatic loss will assist families who are grieving and encourage them to "choose life." Carol is an administrative assistant. She resides in Ontario with her husband.

- **Helen Jay** deeply believes that, in order to enable healing, personal experiences of loss should be shared. Following the sudden death of her son, Adrian, several life-changing events occurred for her family, inspiring Helen to write articles about grief and about coping with the traumatic death of a child. A retired registered nurse born and educated in Nova Scotia, Helen—as a volunteer facilitator—offers one-on-one support within Bereaved Families of Ontario (Midwestern Region) and Wellington Hospice. Emotional survival and eventual reconciliation is Helen's goal, for herself and for all those who struggle with loss. Helen lives in Ontario with her husband, John.

- **Janet Rice** was born and raised in the Maritimes, and has lived her adult life in southern Ontario. She has always had a special interest in music. After leaving her career as an elementary-school teacher to raise her sons, Janet taught private music lessons in her home studio; she has also participated in choirs and ensembles, including a swing band. Following the tragic death of her thirty-six-year-old son, David, in 2009, Janet became involved in bereavement services. She is a passionate advocate for improved support for those suffering with mental illness.

- **Beverley Ogus** lost her nineteen-year-old son, Russell, to suicide in 1989. A Registered Nurse whose main focus has been psychiatry, Beverley spent many years searching for meaning in Russell's tragic loss. She became devoted to channelling her sadness in helping others cope with bereavement. Returning to school to complete her education in psychoanalytic psychother- apy, Beverley began her own practice in 2000. Today she continues to help her clients who are dealing with the deaths of their loved ones and also those clients who are coping with life's varying challenges.

- **Kathleen Stevens** was a direct-support volunteer with Bereaved Families of Ontario-York Region until the death of her husband, Robert, in January 2015. This essential work became a part of Kathleen's grief journey following the death of her son, Sean, in 2012. By refusing to give up, Kathleen has discovered a posi- tive path: reading, writing, and reaching out for guid- ance. In sharing Sean's story, she honours her son while giving hope to others.

- **Susan Massey** is a personal support worker special- izing in palliative care. The 2008 murder of her sister Brenda Healey brought her an awareness of the lack of support for victims of homicide. Working with Victim Services of York Region and other community groups, in 2009 Susan co-founded the Remember Me Homicide Support Group. Sue was awarded the Queen's Diamond Jubilee Award in 2012 and the Attorney General's Victim Services Award in 2013. She lives with her family in Newmarket, Ontario.

- **Suzanne (Suzy) Richardson's** daughter, Robin, died suddenly in 2008. Suzy's subsequent grief journey led her to explore bibliotherapy and the importance of reading for bereaved family members. She now researches, sources, and donates books to local groups and agencies to support grieving families. Suzy is a receptionist for the Town of South Bruce Peninsula and lives in Wiarton, Ontario, with her husband, Don, and their two dogs, Shadow and Bentley.

Praise for *"Life Came to a Standstill"*

"In *Life Came to a Standstill*, seven bereaved mothers and one bereaved sibling present their personal reactions to the traumatic and unexpected deaths of their loved ones. Whether the cause of death was homicide, a motor vehicle accident, suicide, or a fatal blood clot, the contributors take the reader into the profound personal and familial devastation following these heartrending fatalities. Born of the penetrating pain of loss, each powerful account illustrates the struggle to survive and the strength of the human spirit as each survivor moves from devastation to regeneration—in the final analysis, choosing to live fully again. This insightful and inspiring collection is an important read for both the bereaved and the professionals working with them."

—Stephen Fleming, PhD, C, Psych., Emeritus Professor & Senior Scholar, Psychology Department, Faculty of Health, York University, Toronto

∞

"Life Came to a Standstill is a collection of remarkably honest and vulnerable accounts of loving, loss, pain, and hope. Each person's story is courageous and candid in approach, which will help the reader to cope with his/her grief after the sudden death of a loved

one. This book validates the experience of loss, provides nuggets of wisdom, and most importantly, provides hope while touching the reader's heart. It is a must-read."

—Christine Goguen, BA, Sociology: Diploma, "Human Services Counselling," Bereavement Services Coordinator, Bereaved Families of Ontario-York Region

∞

"The aim of *Life Came to a Standstill* is to give bereaved parents and siblings, such as myself, the permission to grieve, and to mourn within our own space and time, all the while feeling comfort and support from those who have gone through the tragic experience of losing a child. No one can even begin to describe the pain involved in such a traumatic experience, but the authors of this book have had the courage to map out their grief paths, each in their individual writing style. At some point in their journeys, they have chosen life, in a way that inspires us to do so as well. This is why I find this book so moving: ultimately, it speaks to those of us who want to choose life, but who desperately need the support of those who understand."

—Christine Evain, Assistant Professor, Ecole Centrale de Nantes, France

Printed in Canada